JOSE GASPAR AND OTHER PIRATES

By

P. T. Meharg

This book is a work of non-fiction. Some names have been changed to protect the privacy of individuals. The events and situations are true.

© 2003 by P. T. Meharg. All rights reserved.

No part of this book may be reproduced, stored in a retrieval system, or transmitted by any means, electronic, mechanical, photocopying, recording, or otherwise, without written permission from the author.

ISBN: 1-4107-4602-X (e-book)
ISBN: 1-4107-4601-1 (Paperback)

Library of Congress Control Number: 2003093620

This book is printed on acid free paper.

Printed in the United States of America
Bloomington, IN

1stBooks - rev. 09/17/03

CONTENTS

THE LAW CONCERNING TREASURE HUNTING

United States law regarding Treasure: " Coin, gold, silver plate or similar articles hidden for safe keeping and forgotten or remaining undiscovered by reason of death of the person who hid them, are technically known as Treasure Trove......Treasure Trove is where any money is found in the earth, but not lying upon it, and no man knows to whom it belongs."

In present day terms this includes paper money!

" A finder of treasure trove is entitled thereto, as against the owner of the land where the treasure was found and all the world except the true owner, in the absence of statute, but the owner of the land is entitled to property *other than* treasure trove, embedded in its soil. The owner of the soil in which treasure trove is found acquires no title thereto, by virtue of his ownership of the land ".

To dig for treasure get the landowner's permission--- otherwise you are guilty of trespass! --- in a written agreement that includes:

1. Names of parties searching
2. Reason for searching
3. Agreement on division of treasure

If land is State owned permission must be obtained from the State. Most states do not demand any percentage of the find.

ILLUSTRATIONS

Dedication

This book is dedicated to one of the truest and finest gentlemen I have ever had the pleasure of knowing, Colonel, Robert H. Crockett, also known as the "Colonel". The "Colonel" was an avid Treasure hunter and history buff. He had a four drawer file cabinet filled with credible information concerning treasure, pirates and history. The "Colonel" was my source of the treasure hunting diary kept by George R. Collins of which the "Colonel" referred to as the"Papers", and that are featured in this book. The "Colonel" passed away in 1960 without ever reaching his goal of finding a real "TX".

PREFACE

I was about 10 years old when my Grandfather started telling me stories about some of his experiences on the West Coast of Florida. Granddad moved to the west coast of Florida with his father and brother and their families from Dallas, Texas in 1880. They had a large tract of land on Boca Ciega Bay, in now what is the city of Seminole and on which they had an orange grove and small farm.

His own first endeavor, other than helping the family on the property, was to operate a small sailboat, hauling freight, between Cedar Key and Key West, the largest population centers on the West Coast of Florida. Based on the census of 1880 Cedar Key had 2000 people and Key West had 10304. Tampa had 720 in the same census and Hillsboro County, where the property was located before it became Pinellas, was 5814. He told me many things that spurred my early interest in the history of our area and my greatest regret is that there are only a few things that I can now recall. Granddad died in 1948, when I was 12 and I guess when you are that age only the things that really interest you stay with you in the memory.

One thing that is remembered is a place a few miles off the coast of Hernando County was a thing that Granddad called a "boil", and was where a freshwater spring boiled to the surface. Granddad said that there was fresh water for probably a half mile in every direction from the center. He said he would get fresh water there as did the Spanish when they were on their way back to Spain with gold from Mexico, saying the Spanish would sail the coast to be able to find this spot and as they passed through it would toss buckets with lines to haul them back aboard and in this manner replenish their supply of fresh water. Grandad said they liked this method as they did not even have to stop sailing in order to get all the fresh water they needed. Another place in the Gulf he mentioned and that had always interested him was near Key West, a place he called "White Horse Light" and there, he said, was an oil slick that never went away. He believed that it was natural seepage of oil from a crack in the earth. On a trip to the museum at Cedar Key, with my oldest son, in the mid 60's I saw what I thought was a picture of my Grandfather standing with a boat when it was on the "ways" (dry dock). When I got home I asked my Grandmother what the name of the boat was and she said it was named the "Ida". That is the name of the boat in the picture and I am sure the gentleman next to it was my Grandfather.

When Granddad moved to Seminole the area was pristine and the fish, he said, were so thick in the bay that you could walk on them. He had a dock that went into the bay and if he needed some fish for supper he would walk out on the dock and with his shotgun get all the mullet he needed. Granddad said that when he came to the Seminole area in 1880 that you could still see the damage done by the hurricane of 1848, a span of 32 years. He was told that the storm blew tide water 50 miles up the Hillsboro river and that would put it nearly to Zephyrhills. If we ever have another storm like that I wouldn't want to be around. The shoreline on Boca Ciega Bay where they settled had little or no mangroves along the shore and it was almost a beach like condition. After the storm of 1921 the mangroves took over. I have family pictures from that time and there is only sand where now there is much tree growth. This should be considered as to the condition of the bays and islands at the time of the pirates.

He said that he had met Indians in the woods and they were friendly but seemed lost with no place to go. He helped put the first Rail Road bridge across Long Bayou and while putting down pilings on the East side, at the waters edge, found a burial of Spaniards. They were buried head to toe and still wore their armor. Granddad took a helmet, breastplate and a skull. My Grandmother said she hated the skull, which Granddad had put on the mantle and would, in the summer when the humidity got high, turn green. When my grandparents built their new house, they placed all things not wanted in the old barn and it was set afire. The Spanish artifacts became ashes.

My Grandparents did most of their shopping in Tampa and if you went by boat it was a two day trip and if you went by wagon it became a 5 day ordeal. There was a bridge that spanned a creek that came from Lake Tarpon (then called Lake Butler) that emptied into Tampa Bay North of Safety Harbor and on the West side was a place called Rodger's Station. If you made the trip to Tampa this is where you crossed over to the Tampa side.

Not all of the musings found in this book have a direct connection to treasure but mainly to apprize the reader that Florida has a rich history and that Pirates have a part in that history and were here long before the tourist and land developers. Many of these tales, if not completely factual, are based upon some real event or occurrence.

I was told by the "Colonel" of a cache of about $25,000 found by a fellow, who would later become a treasure hunting partner, in the North part of the bay at some place in the middle of the road. Another treasure hunting buddy told me that he had been up to the Rodger's Station site hunting treasure with this same person and all he did was to look in the middle of the old road. It then started to make sense why he was looking in the middle of the road. This cache was not Pirate loot but probably from the "Prohibition" era. My treasure hunting partner never did mention this cache and would only grin when asked about it. I have searched this area also but never found anything worthwhile but did find 1 Indian Head penny near the surface and at about 18 inches, a Hillsboro County license plate for a car dated 1913. This license plate was well preserved and was all porcelain. I donated it to the Pinellas County Historical Society.

My Grandmother came to Clearwater from Deep Step, Georgia. She was a small lady about 4' 10" but could shoot the head off of a chicken at 100 feet with her 12 guage, "Long Tom" shotgun, (her Mother was half Creek Indian and maybe this why her aim was so good). She and her twin sister came here when they were young and she was raised by the Bailey family and at first lived at Bailey's Bluff also known at the time as Indian Key. She told me of all the arrow heads that she found there. We started going there to search for them and she was right, there were so many that we named the place the "Factory".

Along the shore line there were so many arrow heads you could dip them up with a bucket. There is a natural outcropping of flint there and it is my opinion that the Indians had craftsmen, as we do, to just make arrow points and the points that were there were culls or points not good enough for use or trade. The 1812 U. S. Army chart shows a lot of Indian trails converging at Baily's Bluff. On the map the trails are shown coming from where Jacksonville, Miami and Lake City are now and so I believe that this place was a place to trade goods, an early day "flea market". The owners, who were developing the property, did not like us in the area and brought in a bulldozer and pushed about 2 feet of dirt over the area.

When I was 16, I took to skin diving as a way to recover sunken treasure. With all the stories that I had heard, I believed there would be no problem at all finding all that gold that littered the bottom of Tampa Bay and the Gulf. In the beginning the cost of SCUBA was very high and I did not have the money to get all that I needed but Bill Jackson's, at that time an army surplus store with a small scuba section, would rent them. When a trip was planned I would go to see Bill and he always wanted a deposit for the regulator and tank, but I was always able to spin some sob story to get out of paying the deposit. It always worked. I have always had the greatest respect for Bill and he and his store are class acts. I discovered fairly early that this treasure hunting stuff can get real expensive. No matter what you have, you never have enough or the right equipment for the job at hand.

Before buying any diving gear I tried diving with a hard hat, a thing I don't recommend. Al had been using this kind of diving method for some time having done some diving with Robert and Oliver

Edie long time divers in Tampa Bay. The helmet just kind of sat on your shoulders with a small strap to keep it secure and the air supply was a hand operated wobble pump that someone had to keep working as long as you were down. We decided to make a dive on a boat named the "Vandalia" that had sunk in the bay in the 20's just East of Bahama Shores in South St. Petersburg. I put on the helmet and went overboard in about 8 feet of water. The visibility was real good on this day and as Al kept me in air, I started looking for anything of interest. I found as I was walking around, the engine that powered the ship, the shaft and the propeller. The propellor and the shaft are the only things worth salvaging as the shaft is either stainless or monel, the prop is about 36 inches in diameter and is brass. I saw something that caught my eye on the bottom and without thinking, bent over to pick it up. Not a thing you want to do. You see as soon as my head went down the water started to pour in and I had to get out of this thing as fast as I could as now the helmet was full of water. A successful escaping of this episode, taught me one thing, that to use this "thing" a lot of deep knee bends are required.

I bought my first scuba gear, from Clark & Siviter, a local wholesale distributer, a Diveair, in 1955 and found it superior to anything else that was on the market at the time. My diving partner, Al, bought an Aqualung and we got real serious about this diving for treasure.

We dove a lot of ships, the British Paymasters ship off the Pier, a Confederate gunboat in Tampa Bay, some large boat with canon in Charlotte Harbor and some others really not worth mentioning. The paymasters ship is probably the scariest dive that I made in my treasure hunting endeavors. Robert and Oliver Edie had done salvage on this ship early in the 1930's and did salvage some things of interest and it is said the canon that was in front of the yacht club came from this boat. They used dynamite to blow the boat apart to get at the ballast that was both lead and steel. They made two piles, one was a lead pile and the other was steel. Robert and Oliver had sold must of the lead and since there was little market for the steel it was the biggest pile but there supposedly was some of the lead pile still there. We decided that we could retrieve some of this lead and make a little money. My one trip to this ship was definitely my last. On the surface the visibility was around 5 feet and as I went down it got less and less until at the bottom none at all and the only way you knew that you were there is when you were head first into the mud. I found what I thought was the biggest pile and was looking for the small one when I ran into one of the ribs of the ship. The ribs had the nails sticking out and were very sharp and since they were not visible, it was too easy to swim into one and severely hurt yourself. I had a habit of not wearing a weight belt and in this dive it was a good idea as I had no idea which way was up, so a deep breath of air would give me the direction that I needed to go. After reaching the surface and getting into the boat I saw that my t-shirt that had started out white was now nearly black and whatever the mud was on the bottom would not wash out. Whatever is there it is ok with me that it stay there.

It is said that the small canon that at one time was in front of the St. Petersburg Yacht Club came from this ship.

One thing we found out real early was that a boat of some size was necessary (we did not have one) a good magnetometer (another thing we did not have) and on and on. In 1958 we decided that the smartest and cheapest thing to do was to look on land where the Pirates had buried it rather than in the water where it had sunk. Our first detectors were the old military type for detecting mines (army surplus bought at Bill Jackson's) they were heavy and not too good and the batteries were very hard to come by. The only place that I could find them was at Cooper's, an electronics supplier in St. Pete. Al and I have looked at almost every suspicious location in the Tampa Bay area and found nothing of value.

There was a local "character" who liked to claim that he was a treasure hunter, had great locations and had found plenty of treasure. One of my treasure hunting friends called me one day and suggested that I come and see some gold doubloons that he had just come into his possession. Without hesitation I went to see this find. When I arrived, my friend showed me these coins and something did not look right with them, too gold or something. My friend then dropped one and it broke into pieces, something that a real gold coin would not do. He informed me that he had been hunting treasure with this "character" and he led them right to where these coins were found. My friend really believed that they had hit the real thing. When arriving home and looking at the coins he accidently dropped one of the coins and it shattered, not what the real thing would do. When he confronted this "character" about the coins, he was told that he was being tested to see if he could be trusted. These coins were very good imitations and if he had not used so much Bismuth in the process could have passed for real. Not too much later, Al, my diving partner, called and said to come and see what he had found. When I got to Al's house he showed me some gold doubloons that he had found while hunting along the shore with our "character" and using a palm frond to push away the sea grass found these beautiful coins just conveniently laying on the surface of the sand. Upon looking at these coins they really looked fake and I decided to do the test and I dropped one.

When it hit the floor there was just a dull thud. Picking it up I could see now that it was slightly bent, so I bent it some more by hand and it bent very easy and gold paint stuck to my fingers. This "character" had made them of lead and painted them gold to appear real. My friends are not the only ones taken in by this "character" as I have heard from others who have discovered that he is prone to "salting" areas to get people enthused and to use their money to finance his ideas and expeditions.

I have only been out with this "character" once and that was to retrieve a German Lugar pistol that he said he had lost in the water off Mullet Key. He got us to take him to where he said it was and he assured us that he knew exactly where to look. After about 2 hours in a 16 foot row boat with a heavy load of barnacles and a 7 horse power motor we got where he said he had lost the pistol. We looked from place to place for maybe an hour and his memory kept getting fuzzier and fuzzier until I told him I did not believe that he had lost anything and that this was a wild goose chase, which he did not deny. Said he was testing us. This person is still around and probably is still up to his old tricks. About this time I found that a friend of mine knew someone who had the "Real" information.

Treasure hunting usually is a Siren's song, leading you further and further into her lair. I suppose very few treasure hunters have ever found anything of consequence but they believe that given just one more clue, would be rich beyond their wildest dreams.

This writer has chased those dreams with what I believed was better than average information and clues. I and those with who I have searched and researched, the "Colonel", Ike, Bob, Les, and Al were all of better than average intelligence and our searches revealed there had been "something" buried where the "Papers" led us. Concrete vaults, very large excavations, marks on trees, told us that we were on the right path but late, very late, and as in most cases these excavations were years old.

Some writers would have you believe that our main character "Jose Gaspar" never existed, thought up by some land speculator wanting to sell swamp land to the gullible and having them believe that there was a spectacular treasure buried beneath this valuable parcel of land, or the marketing of some festival in Tampa. The "Papers" detail the hunting of Jose Gaspar's treasures as early as 1865, long before the Florida land boom and the speculators were born or any parades down Tampa's streets.

I have never made a concerted effort to do a lot of formal research on Gasparilla. Many others have already done so and I don't believe that I could discover something that was not already known and written. There are quite a few books that have been written, if the reader needs more biographical information, on wether or not Gasparilla really existed. It is not this writers intent to prove to anyone that Jose' Gaspar was authentic but only to expose the reader to a diary kept by an early treasure hunter who did and with his own research had actual contact with those who had known or had spoken with members of the crew (s) and the people who had searched for these treasures.

The "Papers" are a kind of diary or log written by George R. Collins, a treasure hunter, and contains his search for the treasures secreted along Florida's West Coast. G.R.C., as he is referred to in the book, did it appears, extensive research for the time, having spoken with those having direct or indirect experience with the burial of the treasure or the search for the "TX". G.R.C. is said to have made only two copies of the "Papers", one for himself and one for his long time guide (name unknown). After G.R.C.'s passing his copy of the "Papers"became the property of C. W. Demoy and upon his passing in 1953 became the property of the "Colonel", who in 1959 gave a copy to this writer. Before I was able to see and acquire a copy of this manuscript, I had heard of it, as had most all treasure hunters on the West Coast of Florida, all wanting a copy for themselves. My friend Ike said that if I wanted to see the "Papers" he would call and ask the "Colonel" if it was ok, which was done and the "Colonel" said for me to come on over.

Ike said that there was just one catch to seeing the "Papers" and that before the "Colonel" would show them to me I had to let the "Colonel's" dog "Sonny" kiss me, as the "Colonel" believed that dogs were the best judge of character and that until Sonny kissed me, there would be no looking at the "Papers". The "Colonel" and I had talked for maybe an hour, when from the corner of my eye I saw something headed for me and the next thing I knew I had been kissed. Without another word being spoken the "Colonel" got up and produced the "Papers" for me to read. There had been just a few pages from this diary leaked here and there by parties unknown, and just enough to make you want to see the real thing and here I was now looking at the real thing. The manuscript given to the "Colonel" by C. W. Demoy's wife, had also told a long time treasure hunting associate that she was tired of the whole thing and had burned them. So, as you read this manuscript, see how many stories true and false have followed it around. C. W. Demoy mainly hunted the "Bakers TX" at Lemon Bay with the "Colonel".

There is among the most avid treasure hunter, some form of superstition surrounding treasure hunting and the things that should or should not be done to insure there is no jinx applied to their search. The "Colonel" would have none of us say the word treasure as it would surely be bad luck and to use only the letters "TX". There is also the relying on "authentic" treasure maps. It is the belief of this writer that pirates did not create maps so that others could find their loot as in some kind of scavenger hunt but only as a memory refresher to the location of secreted treasure. Probably the most elaborate authentic treasure maps were created by the pirate or a member of the crew long after the burial of the treasure. Most monies that have been found and made public have been small amounts in pouches, jars, pots and etc. buried near a tree or some kind of mark so the retrieval for the burrier was made easier. These deposits were probably made by crew members and I refer to them as "crew money". Some treasures are also just found by accident.

So, if this manuscript creates a deep desire to search for buried treasures, have fun, enjoy the time out of doors, but remember there have been many before you. I do believe there are some "Txs" left to be found that are mentioned in the "Papers" but now maybe under someone's house or under a parking lot at some shopping center.

So much for progress.

Homestead dock on Boca Ciega Bay around 1915

Granddad around 1940

CHAPTER ONE

RECORD OF GASPARILLA

FROM OLIVER H. PARKER TO JOHN D. KING

(Copied Verbatim)

Gasparilla belonged to the Court of Spain. Was an intelligent man, had access to crown money and jewels, fell out with the Spanish Court, stole a lot of their money, took one of their ships, buried his treasure on the coast of Spain. He was connected with the Spanish Navy. The Spanish Fleet chased him so he came to Cuba and went into the Pirate business. He had a brother in Cuba in the mercantile business to whom he used to take his stolen goods to be sold.

His principal rendezvous was in Charlotte Harbor. Kettle Bay (now Lemon Bay). He first stopped in the mouth of the Manitee river, which is at the end of Tampa Bay. He operated here for about forty years and

captured a great amount of money. He used to make his best hauls from ships carrying gold and silver from Mexico to Spain as he hated his own people more than ever. He also made a big haul that was paid by the U.S.A. to the Dutch Bankers who bought the bonds paid to Napoleon on the Louisiana Purchase, $11,750,000.00 was the amount captured in the latter part of 1818. He had spies out looking for this and his agents found it out by two women lobbyists. Lafitte, the great pirate, posted Gasparilla of the payment. The Dutch ship carrying the money (said to have been the Peacock) is the one which Bell (or Gallagher) was on and Gasparilla gave him the privilege of joining them, which he did.

Gomez, his nephew, then cabin boy, was stolen from his people in Spain, was a Portuguese.

Old John Gomez was a brother - in - law of Gasparilla, having married Gasparilla's sister, as also did Gomez's brother. Gomez was a Portuguese. Old John died on Panther Key, Fla. In July 1900 at the age of 120, by drowning himself. He had $800,000 buried

which he guarded. (He filled every well on Panther Key before he died). He operated with Gasparilla for a long while then Gasparilla fitted him out with a ship and eighteen men and he started out for himself.

On one of his voyages he captured a Spanish vessel out about sixty miles straight out from Boca Grande pass and in the night. He killed all the men as he always hated the Spaniards. It carried considerable treasure and a Spanish Princess who was taking ten Mexican girls back to Spain to put them in a convent to be educated. This was in 1820 or 21. These were taken to a rendezvous in a swamp off Turtle Bay. The girls he scattered among his men telling them to use them. The Princess he tried to get to marry him but she refused and fought him. He told her he would kill her if she did not. She told him do his worst and he cut her head off. She wore a very large and fine necklace worth $100,000 which Gasparilla prized very much. The Princess was buried in a hammock on the north end of a shell mound owned by Oliver H. Parker. Mr. Parker and his brother Will found her grave and dug her up, *finding her head lying to one side. They dug her up in 1902.*

During his time here there came a ship into the Bay one evening and stayed two days. Gasparilla spied her and put his men to watching her. He thought her a man-of war but saw the men carrying something ashore, they made several trips and on the third morning Gasparilla surrounded and captured her, but until he saw there were but twelve men on her. They told Gasparilla they were not pirates but they had $6,000,000 treasure transporting from Mexico to Spain and had conspired among themselves to hide it, scuttle the ship and go to Cuba in their small boats and say they were lost at sea, but if he would spare their lives they would show him where they had buried it, which they did, then Gasparilla killed all of them, thereby adding $6,000,000 more to his ill gotten gains. It is on Gasparilla Island above Boca Grande City. It was put away so nicely that Gasparilla said he would not disturb it. There was a large ships mast found near the Three Sisters Keys, layed up in the forks of the *trees, evidently put there as a mark to the treasure, by Gasparilla. It was found by a man named Wade and two others, was taken, cut up and made into lumber for a small boat. (Cypress mast). The live oaks are profusely marked thereabouts. One of them has a ship cut on it.*

LaFitte was the noted pirate of the coast of Louisiana and the U.S. Government pardoned him for assisting in the capture of an English Man-of-War, during the War of 1812. He disbanded and went to New Orleans as a citizen. (Then went to France). Getting tired of the quiet life after three or four years, he is supposed to have gone to the Yucatan. But he came down and joined Gasparilla with whom he was well acquainted. This was shortly after Gasparilla's brother died, who commanded his second vessel, and was commander of the second ship of Gasparilla's fleet when Gasparilla and all his men were captured.

Gomez, the Cabin Boy, was saved by the men telling the Commodore that the boy was stolen and took no part in the business.

An American Man-of-War cruised up and down the Gulf and was flying an English merchantman flag, with her guns covered. At this time Gasparilla had decided to quit piracy, gather up his treasures and go to Cuba, but he spied this ship as he was returning from up the Manitee River where he had taken up two copper boxes eighteen inches long containing over $200,000. Running into Big Gasparilla Pass, he quickly buried the boxes again, then ran around to Cape Haze, summoned his other ship, saying to hurry as he wanted to make another good haul before he left. Coming about and with a fair wind he hurried out of Boca Grande Pass. The Man-of-War was about six miles out in the Gulf of Mexico. She was running slowly for the purpose of decoying him out which they had been trying to do for four years.

As Gasparilla drew near he got in the bow of his ship and waved a bunch of letters at the ship, they hove to and Gasparilla ran up and was just ready to throw the grapple, when his black flag was run up (evidently prematurely). The other ship then ran up

the American Flag, uncovered her guns and the fight was begun at close range. Gasparilla was wounded, and his second ship, commanded by LaFitte, following about a half a mile, turned and ran back into the bay. Gasparilla seeing this and knowing he was lost, tied a piece of iron around his body and rolled overboard. (Gomez, the cabin boy, said his Uncle was so badly wounded that he could not stand up and was down on the deck and got a piece of chain and rolled it around himself and then plunged overboard into the gulf).

At that time the Americans had not yet boarded the pirate but literally shot them to pieces and the pirate surrendered soon after. Gomez was the son of Gasparilla's sister and Gasparilla stole him on one of his trips to Spain, where he seems to have gone more than once, for at one time he had twenty-four copper boxes made which he brought back to Florida for his treasures. The sailors spared John Gomez, cabin boy, but hung all the others Lafitte, instead of staying in the bay where he could dodge the Man-of-War (she was too big a ship to go in there without a pilot and of course could not have gotten one) ran out of Big Gasparilla Pass and up to the Manitee River where the Man-of-War captured him the next morning (at daybreak).

This was in 1824. They captured all but one man, he jumped overboard and swam nearly two miles. This man was an Irishman named Gallagher, but afterward went under the name of Bell. (This is a slight error as a Negro pirate slipped away with Gallagher (Bell) and also swam ashore with him and stayed with him for a time but suddenly disappeared and it is supposed that Gallagher killed the Negro to insure his own safety.)

The hull of Gasparilla's ship layed on Bell Buoy Bar five miles out from Boca Grande Pass, last seen about twelve years ago, (now March 21st 1909) and LaFitte's ship lays about two miles off Manitee River.

BROTHERS

Gasparilla also had a brother with him who commanded one of the vessels and died before LaFitte joined him. He was buried on the mainland about twelve feet north of where the store and post office at Placida (on the C.H.& N.R.R.) now stands (1909) (still the same in 1919) and was found by Mr. James Parker in March 1897. He was a habitual or inveterate smoker and his front teeth were worn away as by constantly holding a pipe. (Was again dug up by O.H. Parker and G.R. Collins and again by John D. King, who took a souvenir.)

PIRATE CONGRESS

About the time the U.S. bought Florida in 1821, from Spain, (price $5,000,000) and about two years after this date, pirates became so alarmed over the combined issues, U.S., France and Spain to break up piracy in the New World and the capture of 22 ships in one year by the U.S. Govt. They held a great congress on an island now known as Sanibel Island, coming from all parts of the coast of Florida to decide whether to disband or continue piracy. They were represented by such notable pirates as Gasparilla, King John

(Portuguese from Miami), Old Caesar from Caesar's Creek (extreme end of Florida near Kayo Largo), John Gomez (brother-in-law of Gasparilla), Hay Hackley from the Caloosahachie River near Punta Rassa, Old Baker, who was afterward captured at Lemon Bay and many others. The were in conference for nearly two months (about 1824). A great many decided to disband while the leading ones decided to stay.

These were all captured in about two years except old John Gomez who skipped to Cuba where he finally killed Spanish Coronel in a gambling house and fled in a small flat-bottomed boat to Key West. This was just after the Civil War. When old Caesar came he brought his treasures with him, $18,000,000, and hid them on the island (Sanibel) or in the water. Bocilla, another noted pirate on Pine Island and another in Lemon Bay. Gonzales, who buried his money near Little Gasparilla Pass, $6,000,000 south end of an island known as Bourne Island.

These old pirates called themselves The Brethren of the Sea. They visited one

another, often helped one another out and never bothered each other's treasures. They knew where each other's treasures were.

GASPARILLA

Gasparilla's treasures amounted to upward of $30,000,000 and is in six different places.

OLD CAESAR

$18,000,000

KING JOHN

$4,000,000 at Miami

OLD BAKER

$3,000,000

Baker planted his money at the North end of Lemon Bay, east side. He was captured on the Gulf side the next morning after burying his treasures within a mile of where he hid them. On the way back to his boat he saw the Govt. Boat straight down on him. So he told his men "we will play the innocent", but the Captain had a

description of him and hung all of them, 18 men, two who lingered behind got away. One of these named Harris came back when he was a very old man and was found in a dying condition near the treasure, but so near dead that all he could do was to point over a little knoll and say "right over there is the biggest pile of money you ever saw, I helped put it there". He died the next morning. (buried in Englewood Cemetery).

He was found by a party hunting these treasures and had gone ashore to cook supper. These hunters were in here for six years and had the first pull at it, but they loved their booze too well to devote much energy to treasure hunting, so found nothing.

Young John Gomez said his uncle had a burying ground on Little Gasparilla Pass, that his uncle had a regular killing day and after he had made all his prisoners do all the work he had on hand he would take them and kill them all at one killing. Said he had seen his uncle kill so many that he was afraid to go about the place.

Any Negroes he captured he took to market, but all the white men he put to death except when it was necessary to replenish his force. He would select a man and give him the privilege of joining them, if they accepted he would ask if they had any relatives aboard, if they had, he would tell them to cut his head off, as a test.

Mrs. Hoye told O. H. Parker is he could ever find Ballast Point he was near the Treasure. Parker was wading along the shore of Pelou Island one day when the tide was very low and saw a little corner of a rock sticking up. Upon examination he found many rocks of all sizes and came to the conclusion that this was Ballast Point where Gasparilla would run up and unload his ballast. The story by Gomez is "they ran into the largest pass down here to an island in front of it. They came into a bight, past a sand flat on the left and rolled the money out on a twenty foot plank, that they were four days preparing the hole and they used ships pumps to keep the water out of the hole while working. They had the whole thing up on boards and when the hole was prepared they pulled the boards out and let the whole thing go in and the mud and slosh ran over it". (Note by Mr. King: I think Mr. Parker misconstrued this statement for those old fellows knew all about the quick-sand and hard-pan strata here. I think the boards referred to were boards they used to hold the slush and sand back and that after they got the Money put away into the vault they pulled up the boards and let the sand and water run over it.)

(Note by GRC: I believe this description from Gomez refers to another deposit they made at what I have called the "trestle place", they had six principal deposits.) The statement of Gomez with the statement that "it" was 100 feet from the waters edge and that the tide covered "it" led Mr. Parker to believe that it was buried in the Bay (Gasparilla).

One morning Mr. Parker told Columbus C. McLeod that he was going to find Ballast Point. They were at Cayo Pelow where McLeod lived. Mr. Parker found the Ballast Point that morning, as already detailed.

Two weeks later he had another attack and told McLeod he was going to locate the Treasure.

Upon this morning the tide was exceedingly low as it gets two or three times a year. Going to Ballast Point he waded in a N. W. direction along the beach pulling his little boat after him and McLeod following along the shore. He noticed a round coral rock about seventeen feet in diameter covered with coon oysters and standing apart by itself about 100 feet from shore, but on a level withe same kind of formation that lines the islands here along the coast line. This rock was 490 feet from Ballast Point. He, thinking it strange this should be out there by itself examined it, the water being low enough for him to look under it, he saw some rocks that, as he expressed it, "don't grow in Florida".(Gomez said these rocks came from The Island of Pines, being of malachite of volcanic origin.) Calling Mr. McLeod to look, McLeod got much excited.

Mr. Parker did not want to remove this cap rock until he could get some capital interested, but nothing would do but

McLeod take it off, so he and Parker cut it off. (They cut off about a third of it) They rodded into it and found in the center at 27 feet depth a square object about 4 x 8 feet and on the outside of this rectangular place it was 30 feet to bed rock. (They did little rodding) Much removing of evidence and misleading sign put up. Then both quit prospecting and years of idle dreams of vast wealth followed, each getting jealous of the other until for one to hear the name of the other person was to add further contempt and hatred uncalled for.

(Note by GRC: I don't believe this place had anything to do with any TX except possibly as a mark. The place was a wonderfully constructed platform made of blocks about four inches thick, about a foot long, all cut on an angle and layed the same way a mosaic floor is layed. The whole an astonishing piece of work and doubtless very ancient. I saw it a few months after Parker and McLeod cut into it, and most of it was intact at that time. Part of it is still doubtless there.)

THE FIRST TRIP

The "Papers" that the "Colonel"had, when we first began to look for "TX"s", would not let them out of his possession at all. As time went by he would allow me to have just one section and that one being the area that we were searching. Just before his passing away in 1960 he gave to me a complete copy, all of which is contained in this book.

The "Colonel and I would sit for hours and discuss each possible treasure location. We drew our own version of what we believed they were trying to describe onto Topographic charts. All this was done to the scale called for in the "Papers" for the first area we had decided to search. Having done this, it was easy to see how the chart, the "Papers" and the pictures agreed. In most cases everything was as it was supposed to be and where it should be. This gave us some confidence that all of this was not the figment of someone's fertile imagination.

The thought of even trying "Psychics" was considered, as one of the "Colonel's" relatives was said to be psychic. We sent to her some pictures we had taken of the area and she did a reading with them. Each picture she did a narrative on what she received. There were such things as arrows whistling by, groans, the clank of sabers and the sounds of many people. She also said that the name

"Chris" came to her and was a part of some crew. Skeletons were also a big part of the readings, being many and describing places where they were buried, some being put with the treasure to guard it. Many people, and probably most treasure hunters, are superstitious about things relating to hunting treasures. The "Colonel" never wanted the word "Treasure" used as he believed it would put some kind of hex on it and that when talking about it, it was only to be called a "TX".

Having never been in this area before I flew to the Coral Creek area and looked to see if any of the marks were visible from the air. Nothing of consequence could be seen but it was very helpful to determine the best way to approach the site. These aerial surveys were also backed up by pictures for future reference. There were few houses in the vicinity then and none on the properties where we were going to search. There were a few houses on the West side of Coral Creek, probably near where the location of the West box on the "Three Pines" suggested there was a deposit.

We began assembling all the necessary items for hunting treasure in Florida, metal detectors, weapons, probe rods, machetes, shovels, a snake bite kit, bug repellant and many other required items.

The "Colonel" had a Fisher Super M-Scope that was capable of very deep penetration of the ground based on the size of the deposit. This machine, with batteries weighed 48 pounds and was probably never designed to be used in heavy undergrowth. This machine was of the old tube type and contained 5 large heavy batteries. When assembled for use it had two poles, which the operator stood in the middle of to carry the machine, with the receiver at one end and the transmitter at the other. This setup did allow for easy balance but the weight was still considerable and not easy to maneuver in underbrush.

Our first trip to hunt the treasures mentioned in the "Papers" was made in August 1959. After convincing our wives we were not crazy and were to soon be immensely wealthy we started our search. This area was to us the most promising and is called the "Bell's Deposit" in the "Papers" and purportedly contains all of the Louisiana Purchase money. Gasparilla is said to have buried it here, at this location, after getting it in 1818. The research I have done does not confirm or refute anything concerning this matter. I have all the letters relating to this transaction on micro- fische but most are in French and they in themselves do not cover anything but the agreement. There are records that state the bonds were retired in 1818 but not to whom paid. There is some belief that the Dutch bankers bought the bonds the early 1800's from France to gain the interest for themselves and the payoff was to them. The records coincidently show that the payoff is nearly what is mentioned in the "Papers" and this is probably an accurate history.

We left early on a Sunday morning heading for the sleepy little fishing village at the mouth of Coral Creek called "Placida" on the shore of Gasparilla Bay. Arriving at around 8 am we found a hidden place to park the car as to not arouse undue attention and promptly unloaded the car and each person with his allotted load, started for the treasure. We made our way through thick brush towards a railroad track that runs through the west end of the Indian Mound that we were going to search. Reaching the track made things much easier for walking and we proceeded towards the mound.

Upon reaching the area at the mound we could see the sand flat behind the mound and in it was an area that appeared to be whiter than the surrounding sand and I said to my partners that was the place where the treasure was buried. When we finally were able to make it to the sand flat the "Colonel" attempted to set up the machine and found there seemed to something wrong with it as it giving the tone that you hear when something is located and the "Colonel believed that there was something wrong with it. I made the suggestion the he move to an area away from this spot and then try to balance the detector. The "Colonel" moved about 50 feet away and was able then to set the machine. As he came back towards this whiter area on the sand flat the detector started the loud tone once again.

Wow, our first attempt at treasure hunting here and we hit it right off. We had hit the "mother lode" or so we thought. We pushed the 7 foot probe down its full length and hit nothing. Since the "Papers" said it was 10 feet down and covered with a big flat rock, we decided to dig a 3 foot hole and then probe to reach the 10 foot depth. While digging this hole we discovered that just under that white sand was the blackest, oiliest dirt I had ever seen. In the process of getting the dirt out of the hole we hit a piece of wood that had dovetail slots on each end and you could see some kind of writing on it. Upon washing it off we found writing that identified it as a box that had contained dynamite. Once the 3 foot level was reached we re-probed to the length of the rod and hit nothing.

This black dirt and why it was where it was really intrigued this writer, away from this white sand to where normal colored sand was there was just sand down as far as you wanted to dig. I took a sample and had it analyzed at Florida Presbyterian College (now Eckerd College). After testing, Dr. Sqibb said there was a lot of crude oil, an above average of colloidal silver and a lot of iron in the sample.

Hole dug at sand flat with probe rod in it

The mound in front of the sand flat was really overgrown and on our next trip we began the clearing process. To be able to operate the detectors plenty of clear space was needed. The "Colonel" had bought a new, lightweight detector to replace the heavy machine and I had bought a smaller version, the T-10, to cover all the small things that the large detector would miss.

We found an area we believed looked promising and seemed to fit an area mentioned in the "Papers"and began the clearing this part of the mound. As a small section was cleared we ran the machines, just in case we were lucky enough to have cleared the right spot. Nothing was found and we moved to the next likely spot. In the clearing process we did find trees with marks on them, small holes dug and what appeared to be the concrete vault that was called for in the "Papers". This vault was too small to be a cistern for holding rain water, as was done by old time settlers, and also too small to be a septic tank, a thing that did not exist in these parts at the first of the 1800's. The dimensions were about 3' x 4' and 3' deep. It had been opened many years before and therefore contained nothing. It appeared that it had been around 2' below the original ground level and the concrete had shell and Indian pottery mixed in to give it strength.

There was a large Gumbo Limbo tree close to the middle of the mound and at the base of it was a small hole maybe 2 feet deep and when I ran my machine over the area I got a fairly strong reading. I got my 3' probe rod and rodded down til my knuckles were hitting the shell and hit nothing. There was a belief at the time that if something had been there that the detector would read it just as if it were still there. I decided since I had hit nothing with the rod that this must be the case. This tree had all kinds of carving on it. Some carvings had carvings over the top of them and someone had cut their initials Leo and Vic and the date 1906. These names are not mentioned in the "Papers" so I guess that there were others besides those mentioned in the "Papers" that were after this treasure. It is hard to say how long this tree had been here but it did appear to be very old as it was the largest Gumbo Limbo tree, in diameter, that I had ever seen. Looking around at the base of this tree was not at random, as each crew member was paid a portion of whatever the take was and if it happened to be money or jewels, he would bury it near some mark so when he went back he would know where it was. I don't recall many banks in this part of Florida where a Pirate could deposit his loot. In this area, around Gasparilla Bay, I have heard of many small finds buried in clay pots, leather bags or in some cases small wooden boxes. I learned from the manufacturer of the detector that there was no such thing as residue that would set of a machine other than possibly rust, near one of the last trips that I made to the mound area I went back to this large Gumbo Limbo tree to see if there was still a reading and if so I was going to dig down as far as it took to discover what was setting off the detector. When I got to the tree I discovered a large hole where once was only a small one and when I ran the machine over the spot there was no indications at all. I had heard that someone had been to somewhere around here and had found a pot with crew money but the source I felt was not really reliable so there is the possibility that this dummy missed one.

To anybody who has ventured on Indian mounds or islands in Florida especially those that are grown over will recall that mosquitos are numerous and at times unbearable. This mound was no different and the more we cleared the worse they seemed to get. The "Colonel" would operate his machine until there were so many mosquitos on him that when he went to kill them it looked like he was bleeding to death. Mosquito bites never bothered the "Colonel" as the medication that he had to use to reduce the pain from an operation that he had. The "Colonel", at some time in his past, had 5 ribs removed from one side and 4 from the other. When we started this treasure hunting he made it clear to us that if for some reason he fell, we were to make no effort to pick him up, as to do so could break his back. To me, anyone who had to take shots of Demerol and Codeine every 4 hours and still do all that he did on these treasure hunting trips is one hell of a man.

We made many attempts to find the grave of Gasparilla's brother, if nothing else than to prove to ourselves that the "Papers" were accurate and authentic, but we were never able to discover its location. There seems to be some question to wether he was buried on this mound or across the creek to where the "Papers" say the house for the railroad was and still is. The house has always been occupied since I have been going to the area and never made any attempt to try to get permission to hunt on that side of the creek. I do not believe that Gaspar would put his treasure there. The "Papers" say that there are two deposits and allude to the idea that they were buried in a sand flat. There is a sand flat similar to the one behind the Indian mound across the creek and in about the right place to where the diagram with the two boxes are shown some length from the creek. We have never made any attempt to search this one as there were houses very close to it and we felt the fewer people who knew what we were doing the better.

The story about Gaspar's last battle says that it was in the Gulf just off Boca Grande Pass and that he was sunk there. I discussed this with Albert Lowd and he said that he had seen the wreckage of a ship, in the 1930's, when the water was clear and about where Gaspar's was supposed to be. He said that he did know people that had been down to the wreck in the past, at a time when most of it was uncovered and visible. They said that they saw cannon and a large portion of the ship but this was some years before he saw it for himself. This place is about 6 miles out from Boca Grande pass and at a place called "Bell Buoy Bar". The ship has not been seen in many years due to the shifting of the sands and by now most of the wooden parts are gone but probably enough to confirm or refute the claim that it is Gaspar's vessel. Even if it is not, the cannon and whatever else could be salvaged could have real or historic value.

When we started working this spot I really believed that we were at the place that this treasure was buried. I was so sure that I made contact with some pilots with an airline that I had been working as a mechanic to see if they could find a way of disposing of all this gold with as few people knowing about it as possible. This airline had a stop in Havana, Cuba and these fellows made contact with someone there (probably our station agent as he was one of those in charge of the "Bolita" the Cuban lottery and he had the contacts) and said that they could get rid of all that we could supply. The price of gold at that time was $32 per troy ounce and they said we could get $125 on the Black Market in Cuba, not a bad deal. A number of things happened on the way to our being rich, a fellow named "Fidel" appeared and we never found anything to transport.

Now for something else to consider. For those who think that finding the treasure is the only problem. Let us consider the weight of a treasure. The treasure at the sand flat was supposed to be in the amount of $11,620,000.00. The value of gold at the time it was buried was $20.00 per ounce troy (12 oz to the pound). That will give you 581,000 ounces of gold and that then gives you 48,417 pounds and that then gives 24.2 tons of gold. I don't think you can quickly put it in the back of your pick-up and quietly make your departure. Another thing to be considered is the density weight of the gold and if my memory serves me correctly is that 1 square foot of gold is around 1 ton. To dispose of that amount of gold into the market without attracting a lot of unwanted attention is another thing. Problems, problems, problems.

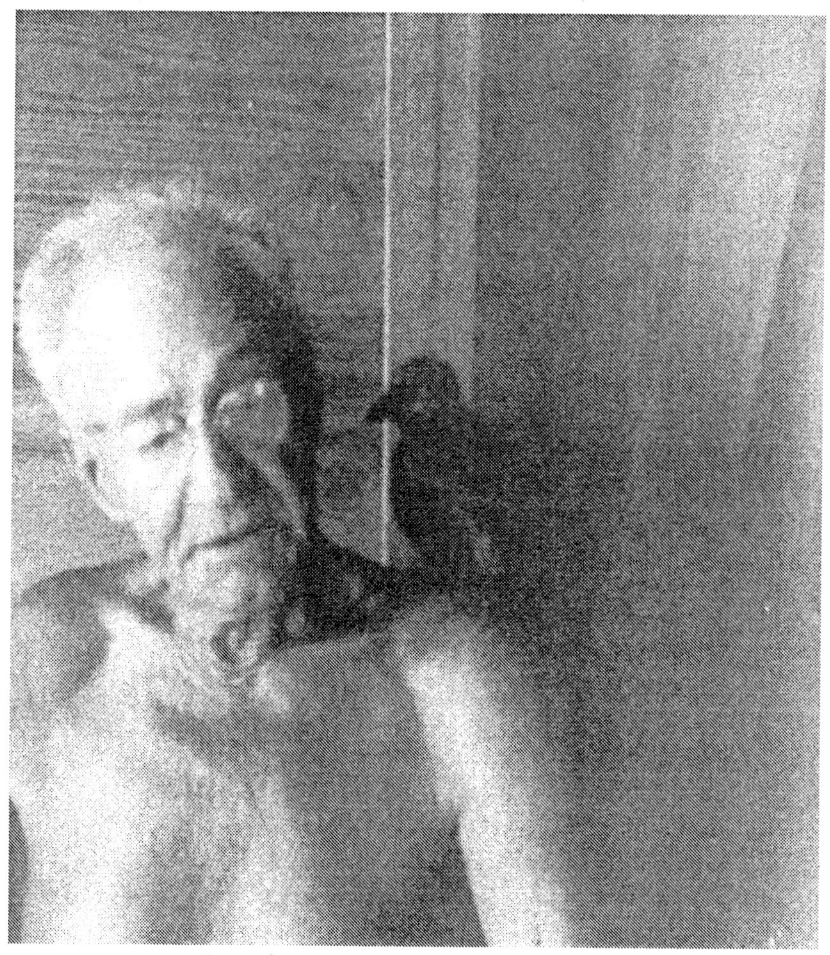

Squires with his pet crow

"Colonel" at sand flat with M-Scope

CHAPTER TWO

GASPARILLA AND MASONRY

The "Colonel", in his files, had some information that led you to believe that Gasparilla had an intense interest in forming a Masonic lodge somewhere on the West Coast of Florida. He supposedly petitioned a Grand Lodge, and the petition was purportedly sent to Atlanta or Charleston. Gasparilla wanted to form a lodge mainly of sailors to be called "The Brethren of the Sea". There is the possibility that Gasparilla already was a Mason and wanted to form a lodge with his own kind of people. The "Colonel" had in his file an ancient pamphlet about the catechism for Masons of that time and is close to the same time period when Gasparilla was young and impressionable. He probably realized most men of stature and probably many ships captains were members of the Masonic fraternity. If, when reading this text, you put yourself as Gasparilla, you might see how he, as a pirate, could bind his men together and to also use phrases and signs to bury and hide his -treasure. As noted in the book, you see that other pirates tried to use, at least the symbol of Masonry as a clue.

TEXT OF AN ANCIENT PAMPHLET

The Grand Mystery of Free-Masons Discovered. Wherein are the several questions put to them at their meetings and installations. As also the Oath, Health, Signs and Points to know each other by as they were found in the custody of a Free-Mason who dyed suddenly. And now published for the information of the Publick. Printed for T. Payne, near Stationers-Hall 1724.

THE CATECHISM

1. Q. Peace be here
   A. I hope there is

2. Q. What a-clock is it
   A. It is going to six or twelve

3. Q. Are you very busy
   A. No

4. Q. Will you give or take
   A. Both; or which you please

5. Q. How go squares
   A. Straight

6. Q. Are you rich or poor
   A. Neither

7. Q. Change me that
   A. I will

8. Q. In the name of, & C, are you a Mason

9. Q. What is a Mason
   A. A man begot of a man, born of a woman, Brother to a King

10. Q. What is a fellow
    A. A companion of a Prince

11. Q. How shall I know that you are a Free-Mason

A. By Signs, Tokens and Points of my entry

12. Q. Which is the point of your entry

A. I hear and conceal, under penalty of having my throat cut, or my tongue pulled out of my head

13. Q. Where were you made a Free-Mason

A. In a just and perfect lodge

14. Q. How many make a lodge

A. God and the Square with five or seven right or perfect Masons, on the highest mountains or the lowest valleys in the world.

15. Q. Why do Odds make a lodge

A. Because all Odds are to mens advantage

16. Q. What lodge are you of
A. The lodge of St. John

17. Q. How does it stand
A. Perfect East and West as all Temples do

18. Q. Where is the Masons Point
A. At the East window, waiting at the rising of the Sun, to set his men at work

19. Q. Where is the Wardens point
A. At the West window, waiting at the setting of the Sun, to dismiss the Entered Apprentice

20. Q. Who governs and rules the lodge and is Master of it
A. Irah }
} or the Right Pillar
Jachin }

21. Q. How is it governed
A. Of square and rule

22. Q. Have you the key of the Lodge
A. Yes, I have

23. Q. What is its virtue
A. To open and shut, and shut and open

24. Q. Where do you keep it
A. In an Ivory box, between my tongue and my teeth or within my heart, where all my secrets are kept.

25. Q. Have you the chain to the key
A. Yes, I have

26. Q. How long is it
A. As long as from my tongue to my heart

27. Q. How many precious Jewels
A. Three; a square Asher, a Diamond, and a Square

28. Q. How many Lights

A. Three; a Right East, South and West

29. Q. What do they represent
A. The Three Persons; Father, Son and Holy Ghost

30. Q. How many Pillars
A. Two; Jachin and Boaz

31. Q. What do they represent
A. A Strength and Stability of the Church in all ages

32. Q. How many Angles in St, Johns Lodge
A. Four bordering on Squares

33. Q. How is the Meridian found out
A. When the Sun leaves the South and breaks in at the West–End of the Lodge

34. Q. In what part of the Temple was the Lodge kept

A. In Solomons Porch, at the West–End of the Temple, where the two Pillars were set up

35. Q. How many belong to a Right Mason

A. Three

36. Q. Give me the solution

A. I will□ The Right Worshipful Master and Worshipful Fellows of the Right Worshipful Lodge from whence I came, greet you well. That Great God to us greeting, be at this greeting, be at this our meeting, and with the Right Worshipful Lodge from whence you came, and you are.

37. Q. Give me the Jerusalem word

A. Giblin

38. Q. Give me the Universal word

A. Boaz

39. Q. Right, Brother of ours, your name
A. N. or M.
Welcome Brother M. or N. to our Society

40. Q. How many particular points pertain to a Free-Mason
A. Three; Fraternity, Fidelity, and Tacity

41. Q. What do they represent
A. Brotherly love, Relief and Truth among all Right Masons; for all Masons were ordain□d at the building of the Tower of Babel and at the Temple of Jerusalem.

42. Q. How many proper Points
A. Five; Foot to Foot, Knee to Knee, Hand to Hand, Heart to Heart and Ear to Ear

43. Q. Whence is an Arch derived

A. From Architecture

44. Q. How many orders in Architecture
A. Five; The Tuscan, Doric, Ionic, Corinthian and composite

45. Q. What do they answer
A. They answer to the Base, Perpendicular, Diameter, Circumference, and Square

46. Q. What is the Right Word or Right Point of a Mason
A. Adieu

END OF CATECHISM

CHAPTER THREE

BELL'S DEPOSIT

Information told G. R. C. by David W. Gillett in 1906
(Copied verbatim as written at that time)

Four or five cabbage trees in a bunch, in center is an old pine stump. Stump is between two palms on the North side of the bunch, now level with or below ground, in Steel's yard, about 40 or 50 feet East of the house. (Meaning the Placida House.)

Old Gasparilla's $11,000,000 is in 11 copper kegs. Large lightwood stump right on the beach on the mainland side, (100 or 150 yards or less) threw out ballast at stump on sand flat. Tree was blazed on side away from water, other blazed trees ran to stump. In gopher hole saw grass pond about 50 yards from up the beach and another grass pond a little East of South about 100 yards from stump and an alligator hole at pond. (Said he got attraction there)

Concrete about a little West of South 150 or 200 yards in a little patch of palmettos. Gomez (Tampa) stood on stump in woods about 150 yards from stump, a little East of South and close to alligator hole and from there saw the deposit had not been disturbed. (Anderson and Tuck Richards)

BELL

Go in creek below coral rocks (a creek that first flows Southeast) then leave a high shell mound on the left hand side as you go in the creek and pass around it to a small sand flat where the water is some deeper and go into a bend on the left hand side immediately after passing the shell mound above referred to and you are right close to it and there is a mint of it. Bell died at Pensacola, Mr. Gillett wrote and found out. Bell and a Negro got away and Bell stopped at Coopers house and after five days told Cooper and offered to share with Cooper, who agreed and Cooper's wife cooked up provisions for a week but as they were ready to start the Seminole Indians got to killing so they gave it up for the time, intending to go later.

Gomez (John of Tampa) was captured on his uncle's vessel and taken to Tampa by the Navy. He grew up around Tampa and St. Augustine, and was a fisherman at Tampa and there David W. Gillett got acquainted with him in 1848, and intimately knew him till he died. Gillett took no stock in any tales until Tampa men whom Gomez had told dug up $150,000 on Pepper Key. Gomez for a time lived with a daughter of Mr. Huff on Lemon Bay and several times brought her jewelry which she was obliged to sell to tourists because of being poor. She and her husband (name not remembered by Mr. Gillett) afterward died in Ft. Myers.

Gomez came down on one trip with Tuck Richards and brother Frank, Mr. Anderson, and another or two, but owing to threats of Anderson (while drunk) Gomez was afraid to show the place as he thought they would kill him as soon as they learned his secret. They landed at the old pine stump that stands right at the waters edge about two miles North of Coral Creek. Gomez offered to bring Mr. Gillett down but died soon after, but described it to Mr. Gillett as above.

Mr. Gillett was at Gomez' supposed location with Tuck Richards.

Statement of Mrs. Harriet Selner, Gulf City, Fla.
Made to G. R. C. and Mrs. Lizzie Gonzales
May 10th, 1919

Mrs. Selner is the widow of Henry Selner, a pioneer of the Florida West Coast who lived all his life along the coast South of Tampa, most of the time at Sarasota and Gulf City, near where he is buried. The present family consists of Mrs. Selner and two sons Henry and Robert, the latter married. Their home place being a tropical place of such rustic beauty, so primitive and tropical that it can hardly be described.

By Mrs. Selner:

In June 1865 we went in a small sail boat to Coral Creek. The party consisted of Mr. Selner, Mr. Cooper, Mr. Collar, Mrs. Cooper (afterward Mrs. Hoye), Lizzie Cooper and myself. We went ashore at Coral Creek near a mangrove island where there was a small sand flat on the right. There were two oak trees on one which there was finger pointing. There were some marked pines in the woods on one of which there were three letters cut. There was a small flat pond surrounded by small palmetto trees close to where we landed. I believe there is a deposit of ship irons including the iron plates that are flat and with rings in one end for fastening on the side of a ship to fasten rigging to. I believe there are some rocks along the beach of the creek.

Two lines should be run, one from the finger pointing to the pine trees and one from the rocks to the pine trees.

Course: E. by S. of tree
or
W. by N. of pines

Go to the pines (I told her I knew where to find them) then go to the creek and hunt the oaks. That was so long ago they may be gone now though you might find where the stumps were. (I found them, they are there now) I believe the ship irons are E. by S. of the oak tree. Mr. Collar found the rocks on the beach which were in the description, so I heard him say that night or the next day while we were at the creek. I think the irons are on the line from the oaks to the pines. (They are exactly so) The finger points East. (More to the South) (The finger points to about where the rocks probably were.) I believe the treasure is buried on the line from the oaks to the pines. I remember that it is buried twenty paces from one of the points. (She first said forty, then after talking with Mrs. Gonzales the "twenty" seemed to come to her.)

I think there are two deposits, one on each of the two lines. We anchored and went ashore where there is a little sand beach and to the South or East is the pond. The ship irons are E. by S. of the oak tree with the finger pointing. Draw a line from the three pines to the oaks. The small pond surrounded by the palmettos is sometimes dry.

The evening we got there Mr. Cooper went to shoot a deer and as he shot, Mr. Selner was in line and got one of the balls in his breast, injuring him so badly that Mr. Cooper had to carry him to the boat. (Mrs. Gonzales still has the gun.)

They worked all night with Mr. Selner to get the blood stopped and the next day started back with him to get necessary medical attention. Mr. Selner recovered, but that was the last time any of them ever made an effort to go there. Mr. Collar possibly saw the rocks that day before they started back, either the evening before or that day.

(Mr. Parker showed G.R.C. where a man named Anderson showed Mr. Parker where he had found a pile of rocks and moved them. It seems that Anderson had a part of the story relating to the rocks, but very likely nothing else, for that seems to be all that he hunted. Mr. Ellis hunted the pile of rocks for twenty years at the waters edge and never hunted anything else and told Mr. Parker if he could find the rocks he could go straight to the money. It is supposed Collar

told Ellis, but Ellis always hunted the opposite side of Coral Creek. (Evidently Anderson knew nothing of the finger pointing, for he nor anyone else told Mr. Parker of it and Mrs. Selner seems to be the only one who possessed that information.) Mrs. Selner said that W. G. Stephens, Parish, Fla. Has some information and to go see him. He told her it was so near Mr. Parkers house that he could do nothing. Stephens is a section foreman of the S. A. Line. She said to tell him Mrs. Selner sent me. Mrs. Selner said that Bell first started for there with Cooper and were stopped by an Indian raid. Bell had disappeared by the time of the trip in 1865. No other trips were made by any of them. Bell came to Cooper's with a large sail boat, anchored, made arrangements for Cooper, Selner, etc. to go with him, went away to be gone a short time and never returned. His vessel layed where he had anchored it for several years till it sunk. (This is evidently when he died as investigated by Ellis.) Mrs. Selner does not know of Ellis, doesn't remember of hearing of him. I asked her. She had never heard of the time or the place of Bell's death. Bell never told them of more than this deposit.

Map made by Mr. David W. Gillett, from memory
May 5th, for Mr. John D. King, at Placida

#1. Represents location of large Beach tree now gone, and upon which was carved in an elaborate manner the designs as shown containing figures, letters, cross and anchor.

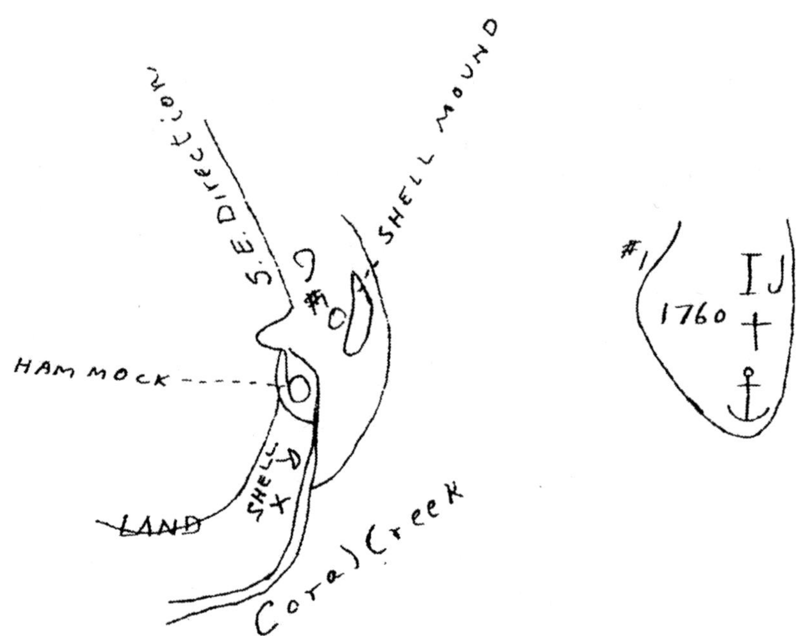

It is said that Mr. Ellis was a soldier in the Seminole War in which Bell (Gallagher) served seemingly with Cooper and Collar. It seems that Mr. Ellis did not have as good a description to the actual location as Cooper did, as he seems to have the best of all. Mr. Ellis spent many periods of several weeks each at Coral Creek and Mr. O. H. Parker got acquainted with him in that manner.

Mr. Parker knew Mr. Ellis from about 1870 to 1890 and by that time Mr. Ellis was too old to come and live out of doors there and hunt it anymore. He many times told Mr. Parker that anyone would be a fool to hunt from the creek (Coral Creek) and that if he could find a circle of stones he could go straight to the treasure. He never hunted anything except the stones and never found them.

Mrs. M. E. Bevill

There is now (1919) a daughter of Mr. Ellis postmistress and station agent at Arredonda and she has a sister named Mrs. Lillie E. Sellers, living at Baxley, Ga. Mrs. Bevill has a son working for the S. A. Line at Palmetto in the freight department. An interview with Mrs. Bevill discloses that Ellis never told any of his family the cause of his trips to Coral Creek. Ellis told Mr. Parker that when he heard that Bell had died he did not believe it and got on a horse and rode the three hundred miles to find out that Bell had died and talked to the family who had taken care of him and also saw his

grave. So it is a positive thing that Bell himself never got away with the treasure.

Statement of Lizzie Cooper, do Hoye, do Mrs. Gonzales West Tampa, Fla., May 10, 1919

When I was a little girl I went with my folks on a boat to Coral Creek, on the trip at which time Henry Selner was accidently shot by my father, Mr. Cooper. I saw him bringing Mr. Selner in the camp after shooting him. I saw them from the deck of the boat. The next day we all came back to Sarasota, where we then lived. That is all I remember of the trip. I have heard Mother say there was a "J" and a "K" on a tree, also a "T". Also there was a tree with a finger pointing on it.

Also, I remember the treasure was buried twenty steps from something, but do not remember what she said it was. I remember that when we went in Coral Creek the boat was anchored in a round kind of place.

Statement of Della Hoye, do Mrs. Deason, now Mrs. Willis, wife of H. S. Willis. Sister of Mrs. Lizzie Gonzales

I often heard mother talk about it but did not pay much attention to what she said, as I had no thoughts about it, but I do remember there was a tree with a finger pointing on it. I never went there. I was not born when Mr. Selner was shot there.

(By GRC: About 300 feet down the stream from the oak with the finger pointing and on the South side of the R. R. trestle, is a small creek, a very small one and in the mouth of it was a pile of rocks which Gomez told Anderson "they" put there as a mark. Probably this is the pile of rocks Mrs. Selner refers to. Robinson told Mr. Parker that he moved them. It is also about 300 feet from where the irons were found. The flat plates spoken of by Mrs. Selner were made into plow points by a farmer. G.R.C. has a mast yoke from the lot of irons. Got it in 1894.)

Tree with finger pointing

Tree with ship cut on it

CHARLOTTE HARBOR

Sometime before the turn of the 18th century Gaspar appears to have decided to relocate to Charlotte Harbor. Charlotte Harbor was a secluded, placid body of water with a deep water pass in front of it. Many islands with all sorts of birds and waters teeming with fish, this uninhabited area must have been a paradise and great hiding place for Gaspar.

The story goes that Gaspar set his men to building 12 log houses some where on Turtle Bay. Wells were located and gardens planted, all in the general area. On another island the pirate built a stockade to house his prisoners and it is believed that this island is the one now called Captiva, either by coincidence or fact. The pirate not only got riches from his conquests but also fine clothes, food, wines and many other items of comfort. These things needed to be stored and so store houses were built.

The "Papers" really never mention where Gaspar lived when not pursuing treasure but do mention where his brother was buried and that would lead one to believe that he did call Charlotte Harbor home. The pirate knew that the U.S. Navy and probably many others were on the lookout for him and that if possible, they capture him or sink his vessel, so having a safe harbor to hide in especially in so sparsely a populated area had to be appealing.

This harbor was not frequented by the U.S. Navy so they would not have had any knowledge of where the deep water or channels were to be able to navigate this body of water. Gaspar, knowing this, probably felt quite safe here believing that he could defeat anyone who dared challenge him on his own turf.

Many other pirates seemed to have joined Gaspar on the West Coast of Florida, King John, Black Caesar, and others. Who's to say what the reasons were but it does appear it worked to the benefit of all concerned. The "Papers" say that many buried their treasures in the same general location as Gaspar and it is possible that many of the treasure locations and marks belong to someone other than Gaspar.

This writer has covered many of the islands in Charlotte Harbor and if I were a pirate many of the islands would have made an ideal place to call home or to hide loot. One island especially comes to mind, named Patricia Island. This island is quite high and at some time was inhabited, as we found a cistern and what was left of a windmill. The island is covered with St. Augustine grass, many gopher tortoises and citrus trees of many variety. To both east and west of the island is deep water, where the dock was, on the west side, close to the island. We have worked the island to some degree but I must admit it was really hit and miss, mainly because we had no definite information to rely on. I have been told there is now a large home that has been built on the island, so anyone interested in looking there had better talk to the owner first.

Useppa Island is probably where the house of the Admiral was located and seems to have been inhabited from nearly the time of the pirate. One strange thing is where the dock is now located, it is on the west side, where the shallowest water is. All the old charts show the deep water on the east side. The Indians must have realized this as all of the mounds are on this side. This island is truly a beautiful place and to all the past and present owners they really deserve praise for the present condition of it. This is another of the islands that at the time of the pirates did have a free flowing well on its west side, located a little south of where the dock is now. There is a story that has been around for a long time that a treasure was taken from somewhere close to this well.

I had a friend who worked for the Department of the Interior, who owns and controlled many of the islands in Charlotte Harbor, and lived on Sanibel Island. He has told me some of the local histories he has discovered. One is that there is a fresh water creek that is on the island and could be one of the reasons that the pirate "Congress" was held on Sanibel. If this is the island and a "Congress" was really held, it probably would be on some high ground somewhere close to this creek. I believe there is a park now in the area and if some archaeologist looked for this high ground, he would probably find some artifacts of this occasion. One of the pirates supposedly buried his treasure on the island or in the water. A fresh water creek would be an excellent mark. In the "Papers" one of the stories is that they hid the treasure in "clean yellow sand" and so I asked Tom if he was aware of anyplace around Charlotte Harbor that had "clean yellow sand. He said that he was unaware of any place in or on Charlotte Harbor that had it. He did say that he was aware of one island that did, Hoars Island. This island is just south of Marco Island and is made up of the yellow sand. Tom believes that the island is also the highest on the west coast of Florida.

The history, what there is of it, says that Gaspar began his piracy sometime around 1789 and shortly after that chose Charlotte Harbor for his hideout. Records show that the average pirate would manage 12 captures a year. Let us consider Gaspar an average pirate and that he was in Charlotte Harbor in 1800 and sunk in 1824. This time frame gives him 24 years of piracy and at 12 captures a year makes 288 for the time he was here. Let us make another assumption that not all captured vessels had gold or silver but only other types of goods that had value but would not be the kind to bury, these being 50 percent so that leaves 144 to be buried or hidden.

The "Papers" really only mention a few and with so many to bury it is possible that many islands do or did contain buried treasure. Going back to "Hoars Island", it is entirely possible that it is the place spoken of where it is in "clean yellow sand". I have never been to this island and now with its proximity to Marco Island, it is now probably populated.

Another island that very interesting and is not mentioned is Pine Island, but still could have been in the "Papers" under another name. One of my treasure hunting partners wife was born on the island at Pineland and her father started the town of Bokeelia. The only gold I know of as a fact was found here, a small Portugese coin found by Les on the Indian mound at Pineland. The Indian mound here is stepped, just as the pyramids on the Yucatan and Mexico City. I am not sure how the pyramids are aligned in Mexico but this one is facing west and must have had some significance for the Indians. Most of the mounds are on the north end and other than this one, they look like most kitchen middens (garbage heaps). There was one mound in the middle of the north end made of dirt and not shell, that must have been a burial mound and as it had worn away it left bones sticking from the dirt. We never dug at this mound and when we went back some years later, to work the detectors, the mound was completely gone. Another conical shaped mound in the middle of the island has a large house at the top and commands an impressive view. I can't believe that if pirates were anywhere around here that they would pass up an island like this.

Just a passing coincidence, a number of inventors that had the ability to develop metal detectors and may have done so were Thomas Edison who lived in Ft. Myers and Burgess, of Burgess batteries, who lived and had a small laboratory on an island just east of Bokeelia and probably more than these notable inventors have lived or frequented this area. I have never heard that either of these gentleman had any interest in treasure but then very few people are not keenly interested in lost treasure, if for nothing else than the challenge and science in itself is a challenge in the form of search and discovery.

Another thing that probably deserves mention is that Charlotte Harbor and Tampa Bay are very similar, being nearly the same size, shape and having rivers at nearly the same places. It appears that Gaspar preferred Charlotte Harbor while a fellow pirate LaFitte preferred Tampa Bay. Lafitte did frequent the north of Tampa Bay around what is now Philippi Park. It is rumored that Philippi himself was an acquaintance of Lafitte and supposedly grew provisions and boiled saltwater down for salt for supply to the pirate. As mentioned later in this book, are the remains of some vessel located just off Philippi Park There may be some truth to the boiling of water to get salt story. Before the park was completed I found many old bricks along the shore that appeared to have been from a kiln or chimney. This area seems to have been populated from the time of the Indians and DeSoto until this day. There is some history that there was a Spanish Mission to the west of the park and at a place called the Seven Oaks have been found items from DeSoto's time. Near to the Seven Oaks is a Kapok tree that is very old and was here when the settlers got here and saw it. These trees are not native to Florida or even North America but are native to tropical Asia. The fruit pods have fibers that protect the seeds that can be used the same as cotton and the seeds themselves contain an oil used to make soap. Both of these items from the tree are necessary for any explorer or settler planning to spend a lot of time in the area. The question is, how and why did it get here and who brought it?

Near our old homestead on Boca Ciega Bay was an island we called "Cotton Island". It was off this island we swam and gathered scallops. The island was covered with cotton plants that still produced cotton and it was believed that a ship carrying cotton bales was wrecked by a big storm and the bales washed up on this island. If this scenario is correct the bales would have to have crossed the barrier island, so why wasn't the barrier island and other islands in the vicinity covered by cotton from this wreck and not only this one small island. This island had the cotton on it when my ancestors came in 1880, so the wreck, if it was a wreck, had to have been before 1880. It could be possible that someone actually planted the island sometime in the distant past. "Cotton Island" is now infested with condominiums.

Author at sand flat

Bedrock depth at sand flat

Hole in mound with concrete vault

CHAPTER FOUR

THREE PINE TREES CORAL CREEK

These three trees have always been connected with the story of the bullion which was paid by the U.S. to Holland in payment of the debt incurred for the purchase of Louisiana in 1818. They were first described by Bell

(Gallagher) who first told Mrs. Cooper (Hoye) when she asked Bell how he would ever know when he had gone far enough South to be near the TX. He said he would know the place by the markings they had cut in three large pine trees standing in the form of a triangle and has described the markings, she said in later years that there was a "J' and a "K" on a tree and also a "T". (All of which there were.) Also Bell described the tree with the finger pointing and gave the compass directions and the course given by him leads directly between the pines and the tree with the finger pointing.

(Lines run by G.R.C. and O.H. Parker in 1919.)

The Seminole Indian troubles kept whites out of the country and the next heard of the trees was when a Preacher, going across the country on horse back after the Civil War saw them and told of it. The next time they seem to have been seen was when hunted for by James A. and Oliver H. Parker about 1890 at which time they found them. They kept the secret and in 1894 showed them to G.R.C. who at the time made a copy of the markings. At that date the trees were in perfect condition and the markings had not been disturbed or cut into. Soon after they showed the marks to their brother David, who got intoxicated, and told the secret and it soon became nosed about. Hunters went in there and chopped into the markings like fools and have nearly destroyed them, though with a diagram showing how they originally looked they can be traced on two of the trees. One of them has been cut down and is gone.

In 1894 and for about ten years thereafter these markings remained as clear as shown

here. The circle of course represents the round body of the tree and there was a blaze on each of the four sides as represented here, not however the letters N. S. E. W.

The West blaze was a double blaze as represented. (By G.R.C.: The letters can mean "Key for Treasure" or they can represent the amount of the bullion, which was $11,620,000. Namely, K is the eleventh letter of the alphabet, F is the sixth letter and T is the twentieth letter.)

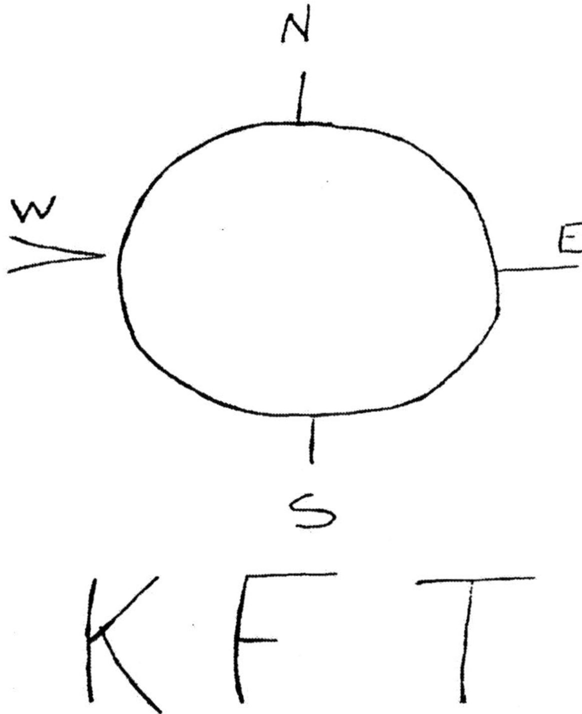
N
W
E
S
KFT

P. T. Meharg

Survey of "Bell" location and description Coral Creek

11. KFT

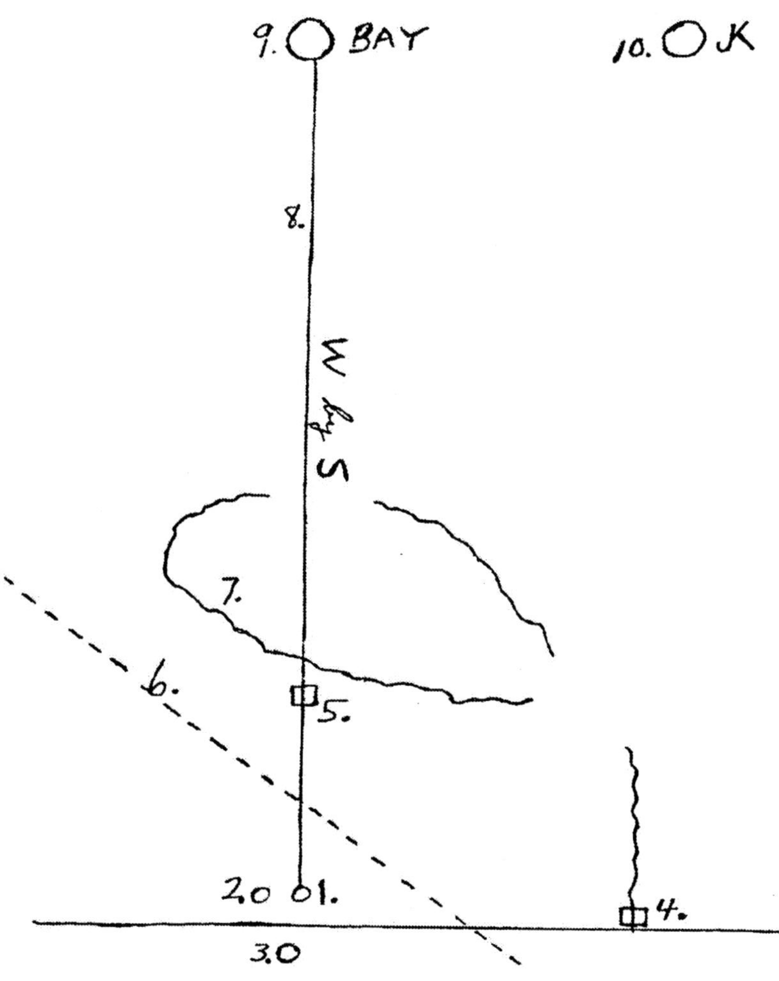

1. *Tree with finger pointing nearly South.*
2. *Tree (oak) with very large blaze on West side toward creek.*
3. *Large Black Mangrove tree standing in Coral Creek.*
4. *Supposed location of rocks found by Collar.*
5. *Where ship irons were found buried just below surface.*
6. *Line of C. H. & N. R. R.*
7. *Outline of pond*
8. *Line run by G.R.C. and Parker (approximately 1000 feet).*
9. *Old pine marked with little bay and creek.*
10. *Old pine marked with J.K. etc.*
11. *Location where old pine stood with "K.F.T."*

Surveyed May 17, 1919 with Mariners Compass

In this marking the two boxes shown at the end of the lines drawn were carved

around the sides of the tree, seemingly to make it possible to show a length of a line so as to designate the boxes at some distance from the creek (Coral) of which the carving is plainly a chart as it shows the two little in the mouth of the creek where it empties into Gasparilla Bay. The three mangrove islands are shown by the three dotted round islands, all five still being there. Carved lines led to the two square boxes.

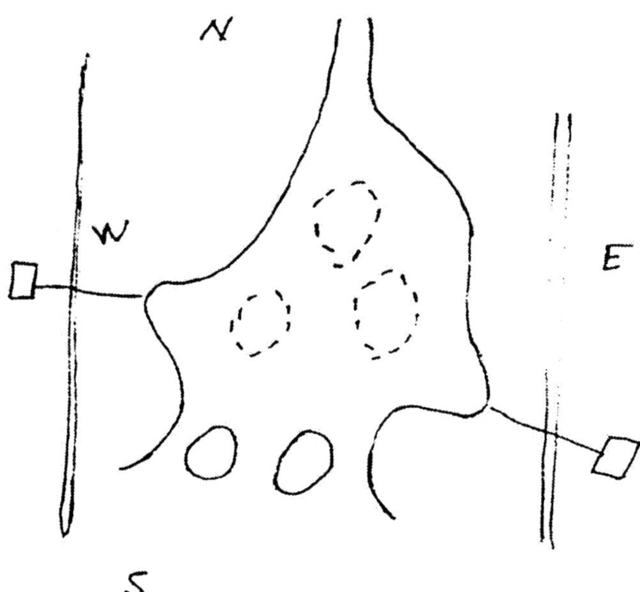

This is the tree that had the marks Bell called the "J" and the "K" but it represents the territory of Coral Creek when viewed as being inverted. (The N.S.E.W. are not carved on the tree.) The line running from the bottom of the "K" is identical with a line of blazed trees running to three small coral islands near the shore in Gasparilla Bay about a half a mile or less to the West. The two small bunches of dots, three each, probably represent groups of trees, likely palmettos as they frequently grow that way. Many palmettos have grown up around there in the past hundred years so these are not easily identified.

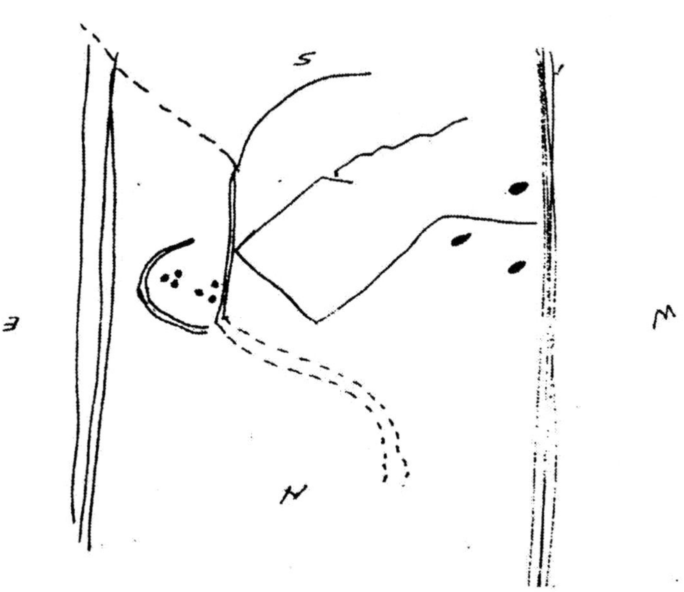
S
E
W
N

CORAL CREEK

The deposit that was called "Bell's Deposit" always seemed to us be the best to search for as it appeared to have the most information connected to it.

The sand flat that we had searched previously still beckoned but now believed that the "TK" must be deeper than the ten feet mentioned in the "Papers". We engineered a jet pump to be able to reach greater depths to completely explore this site and reach whatever was giving this positive indication that something was hidden here. A positive displacement pump was used to supply the pressure and it was driven by a two horsepower engine. A garden hose was connected to six foot lengths of 1/4 inch galvanized pipe and when we made our first attempt to jet down the first section of pipe the hose could not stand this amount of pressure and blew up. This trip needless to say was less than fruitful. Knowing now that a regular garden hose would never stand the pressure I began to look around and was able to find a garden hose a Montgomery-Ward that would stand 500 psi and figured that we were not going to produce any more pressure than that. We now made arrangements to return to the sand flat soon after acquiring the new hose. We set up as before and the new hose worked perfectly and the working pressure probably neared the limit of the hose as it became very ridged, but we were now able to jet all the six foot sections of the pipe to what we believed was the bed rock.

On then day that the jet was brought to the sand flat we had added a new person to our crew as the "Colonel" had passed away and our new member, Les, had never been here before and had no clue to where it was we were going to look. Les had been toying with and old method of detecting metal and that was with a pair of coat hanger wires bent so that they made a ninety degree angle and held in the hand. I guess this is a way to "Douse" for treasure rather than for water. Before we set up for anything we turned Les loose in the sand flat and before long the wires crossed and working as they should were directly over the spot we believed the "TX" was buried.

We had been away from the sand flat long enough that there was no evidence where we had been looking so Les could not have had a clue as to where to look. Now with this endorsement that we had the right place we set up the jet pump and began in earnest to find our treasure. We had jetted down to around 10 feet and we washed out a oak leaf that looked nearly new and next was a piece of some piece of rusty metal that was picked up on the magnet that was being held where the sand was being washed from the hole. We continued down until at 34 ½ feet we hit what we believe is bedrock.

The pipe was hammered up and down to jam whatever was there in the end of the pipe to see just what it was we were hitting. With the pipe out of the hole what was in the end appeared to be grey clay with small rocks in it. To us this appeared to be something natural rather that something made by man. We jetted many more holes and all stopped at the same depth, so we concluded that we had not missed anything that could have been buried and be resting on the bedrock. We last returned in 1965 with a 4 inch casing designed to retrieve some of the substance at 34 ½ feet to prove to ourselves that it either was or wasn't bedrock. The pipe was jetted down and as with some designs, they don't work and this one got stuck fast when nearly to the right depth. We removed the last section of pipe and just left the rest buried.

While we worked in this area some time was spent looking within a half mile radius of the mound and sand flat. A lot of evidence was found of someone being here before us. This area had been logged for the pines and could have been the loggers who left behind the items we found. Many bullet casings were found of different calibers, some being 36, 41, and 44 along with shotgun shells of all calibers. Pieces of dishware and one piece of gold, a cuff stud made by Krementz. By coincidence that year I had received a set of cuff links for Christmas made by Krementz and inside the box was a brief history of Krementz, and their history said that they started to gold plate in 1866 and the stud I had found was plated, so with no doubt it was not left there by the pirates.

On the East side of Coral Creek and maybe a half mile up the creek from the mound there is a place that appears to have been dug from the side of the creek. The bank was somewhat higher than the surrounding land and was not very overgrown. It truly was an interesting place and we ran the detectors in areas where if I were a pirate I would have buried something. The were no marks and there were no large trees, just the higher ground and a lot of scrub oaks. Someone, in my estimation, did dig this place but who or when is doubtful. There was a lot of logging that went on here before and around the 1900's and could have been dug by the loggers but if it was to be a place to bring some larger boat it had to have been before the railroad bridge was built somewhere around 1888. Other than this one trip we have never returned but I do feel that there may still be some kind of small treasure, possibly "crew money" still could be found.

There was a large hole probably 75 feet square and 7-8 feet deep that the owner of the property said was dug for the watering of his cattle. We found no evidence that cattle ever used this pond for watering, no trails no nothing. This hole just happened to be about midway between the mound/sand flat and the three pines. I did work my detector all around this area an got no indications of any metallic objects even though this place is very close to where the ship irons were found. We also spent considerable time looking for any remnants of the ship irons mentioned in the "Papers" and all appear to have been taken or possibly just rusted away.

There was an elderly gentleman and his wife who lived across the road from the area that we were searching and was a very interesting person with many stories to tell about this part of Florida. This gentleman, Mr. Squires, and his wife Ella lived in what he said had been the kitchen of the old Placida House Hotel that once was on the mainland about ½ mile South of the bridge that crosses Coral Creek. The Squires' had a pet crow and the only word that the crow knew was Ella and when hungry would fly around the outside of the house calling "Ella" and continue to do so until fed. The crow had a stiff leg that Squires said was caused by a chicken pecking the leg of the crow when it was young. When the crow would try to land on the top of our car it would slide off due to the inability of it to flex its one leg as birds do when making a landing. Squires also claimed that when some of the executive of the "Old Crow" distillery were fishing at Boca Grande that they heard about the crow and that it was this crow that was pictured on all the "Old Crow" labels on their whisky bottles.

Squires said that he and his father came to South Florida from upstate New York and that they settled somewhere on the Shark River in the Everglades somewhere around the turn of the century (1900). Ella was born and raised on Gasparilla Island. They both knew of the rumored treasures in and around Gasparilla Bay and were able to give first hand knowledge of local lore and treasures and some background of the people involved.

We made a trip to Coral Creek in January 1960 and found that someone had been digging in the creek. We asked Squires what he knew about the digging and he said it was done by some group from St. Pete. He said that he had watched them closely and never saw any results at all. Another person connected with the area said that this group had dug down to 25 feet with a dragline and had retrieved some ballast rock, teak wood and that appeared to be all. I knew of another person who with an earlier group claims to have sunk, using a dragline, a large casing and to have dug out some anchor chain and a skeleton, but another friend who also knew of this person said that he had seen the chain and to him looked just like a chain from a dragline drag bucket. I have never read or heard of anything about any treasure buried in the creek itself that would cause anyone to spend a lot of money to dig in the creek.

The rowboat that was supposedly sunk in the creek and that was full of gold would not require all of that effort (covered below). The story does go back quite a ways as to the digging in Coral Creek. The first record of anyone digging the creek was in 1912 by the Downing Brothers of Tampa. They sunk a wooden casing after building a coffer dam and then sunk a corrugated pipe inside and the story is that they got nothing from Coral Creek but another rumor is that they did find something on the nearby Indian Mound, because they never returned after this episode.

Les, our treasure hunting partner, has a very interesting tale that had happened to him many years ago about a "TX" found somewhere up Coral Creek. He says, as a Captain of a pleasure sailboat in the late 1920's, he came into Gasparilla Bay to escape from some bad weather. While at anchor, he watched as a man rowed out to them from Gasparilla Island.

This man introduced himself and asked if they would like to join he and his wife for dinner, to which Les and the owner agreed. They accompanied the man back to his "house" a place Les could only describe as a shack. Upon entering the house he noticed many things that one would not expect to find in a "Cracker Shack". Les said that there was European pottery, paintings and of all things what the owner claimed was a Stradivarius violin. Les asked where had he gotten all of the items and the man responded that they got them on a trip to Europe. This old man had just butchered and cooked up a hog. All of the meat was ground up like hamburger but according to Les they had never shaved the hair from the hog but just ground it up with the rest of the skin and meat. Les said that it made it hard to attempt to eat without upsetting the host as it was not, to say the least, very appetizing.

After they finished the meal, the man started to tell them of a treasure he had found up Coral Creek. He said that he had dug up enough that he filled a row boat with gold and on the return trip to Gasparilla Island and while still in the creek, the bottom gave way and the boat sank. He said that he made it back to Gasparilla Island and got another of his rowboats and returned for the rest of the treasure. This return trip was successful and made it back to the island. The man said that if he and his father would like, he would take them up the creek and show them where the boat sunk. Les then told the man that the gentleman he was with was not his father but was the owner of the sailboat and that he was just the Captain, for some reason the man then would say no more about the treasure and only wanted to return them to their boat, which he did. It is Les's opinion that the man had to be telling the truth about the treasure he claimed to have found up the creek as there was no way that this person could have afforded the items he saw in the house nor been able to travel to Europe. The boat is probably still on the bottom somewhere up Coral Creek as claimed. We have never made any attempt to locate this treasure as we needed an underwater metal detector and at that time these were very expensive and we could not afford one. Of all the treasures claimed to be associated with the creek I believe that this one is most credible and with the new underwater detectors could be found with a little effort. There may some connection with the place up the creek where the bank has been cut away with this treasure, but I doubt if this old man was responsible.

On another trip to Coral Creek we met a man named Bostick, who claimed to know much about the "Louisiana Purchase TX" and said that it was buried in the middle of the three pines standing in the form of a triangle. He said if he knew where the three had been he could find the treasure. Well, we did not tell him that we did know where the three pine had stood but thanked him for the story. The "papers" never made mention of any treasure buried between the pines but we believed it was worth a shot and a little while later after Bostick was gone, went to where the trees had stood and began to search. Within a short time I had a large hit with the detector and began to believe that this Bostick fellow had some real good information. Probing around with the probe rod I hit something metallic just beneath the surface and we dug to see what it was. In short order we had our answer, a large metal ring possibly for the outer rim of a wagon wheel or a ring to hold together a large wooden water tank. After removing the ring from the area there were no more indications. So much for Bostick's "for sure" treasure location.

I have done what research could be done on a treasure such as this and have complete copy of the Louisiana Purchase on microfiche from the U.S. Archives but almost all of the correspondence and transactions were written in French. I did not feel that there was anything in the agreement that was worth translating that would help finding the treasure as the time between the agreement and the treasure was around fifteen years. I have asked for the date and the place where the payment was made or any records concerning this, but received no response.

As many times as I have been skunked at this place, probably thirty times, I still believe there is something there and that it continues to call me back, but in all probability I will never return.

THE LIBRARY OF CONGRESS

WASHINGTON 25, D. C.

REFERENCE DEPARTMENT
GENERAL REFERENCE AND BIBLIOGRAPHY DIVISION

February 18, 1963

Dear Mr. Meharg:

Your letter postmarked January 27, addressed to the Department of History, has had the attention of this Division.

The first Convention of April 30, 1803, between France and the United States set the price of the Louisiana Purchase at sixty millions of francs ($11,250,000); and the second Convention of the same date provided for the assumption of the United States of claims against France, not to exceed the sum of twenty millions of francs. This sum was regarded as the equivalent of $3,750,000. Concerning these sums, we quote Article 2 of the first Convention and Articles 1, 2, and 3 of the second Convention, which appear respectively on pages 513-514 and 517-518 of volume two of <u>Treaties and Other International Acts of the United States of America</u> (Washington, U. S. Govt. Print. Off., 1931), edited by Hunter Miller:

ART: 2

For the payment of the Sum of Sixty millions of francs mentioned in the preceeding article the United States Shall create a Stock of eleven millions, two hundred and fifty thousand Dollars bearing an interest of Six per cent: per annum payable half yearly in London Amsterdam or Paris amounting by the half year to three hundred and thirty Seven thousand five hundred Dollars according to the proportions which Shall be determined by the french Government to be paid at either place: The principal of the Said Stock to be reimbursed at the treasury of the United States in annual payments of not less than three millions of Dollars each; of which the first payment Shall commence fifteen years after the date of the exchange of ratifications--this Stock Shall be transferred to the Government of France or to Such person or persons as Shall be authorized to receive it in three months at most after the exchange of the ratifications of this treaty and after Louisiana Shall be taken possession of in the name of the Government of the United States.

-2-

ART: 1

The debts due by France to citizens of the United States contracted before the 8th of Vendémiaire ninth year of the French Republic (30th September 1800) Shall be paid according to the following regulations with interest at Six per Cent; to commence from the period when the accounts and vouchers were presented to the French Government.

ART: 2

The debts provided for by the preceding Article are those whose result is comprised in the conjectural note annexed to the present Convention and which with the interest cannot exceed the Sum of twenty millions of Francs. The claims comprised in the Said note which fall within the exceptions of the following articles Shall not be admitted to the benefit of this provision.

ART: 3

The principal and interests of the Said debts Shall be discharged by the United States, by orders drawn by their Minister Plenipotentiary on their treasury, these orders Shall be payable Sixty days after the exchange of ratifications of the Treaty and the Conventions Signed this day, and after possession Shall be given of Louisiana by the Commissaries of France to those of the United-States.

We have found no evidence that these payments involved the actual shipments abroad of currency on the part of the government. Further light upon the matter can only be obtained from the records of the Treasury Department, which are in the National Archives. We are therefore referring your letter to the Diplomatic, Legal and Fiscal Branch, National Archives and Records Service, Washington 25, D. C.

We are also referring your question concerning the existence of a letter from Jose Gaspar to President Monroe to the Library's Manuscript Division.

Very truly yours,

Henry J. Dubester

Henry J. Dubester
Chief
General Reference and
Bibliography Division

Mr. Philip T. Meharg
4130 26th Street, North
St. Petersburg, Florida

HISTORY OF THE NATIONAL LOANS

LOUISIANA SIX PER CENT STOCK

This loan was contracted to pay France for the province of Louisiana, ceded to the United States by that power April 30, 1803. According to the construction of the United States, the cession of France included all the territory now covered by those portions of the states of Alabama and Mississippi which lie south of the thirty-first parallel: by the states of Louisiana, Arkansas, Missouri, Iowa, Minnesota, Oregon, Nebraska, and Kansas: by the territories of Dakota, Montana, Idaho, Washington, and the Indian Territory; and by portions of Colorado and Wyoming. The United States had heavy demands on France for spoliations committed on American commerce during the previous ten years. The amount of these claims was estimated at $5,000,000. The first proposition of the French minister was that the Unite States should pay, for the province of Louisiana, 100,000,000 francs and take upon themselves the payment of the claims for spoliations, but the amount was finally fixed at $15,000,000, of which France was to receive $11,250,000 in United States bonds, payable in fifteen years, and bearing interest at the rate of 6 per cent. The remainder, amounting to $3,750,000, was to be devoted to reimbursing American citizens for French depredations on their commerce. The treaty was confirmed By the Senate of the United States, but was the occasion of an extended debate in the House of Representatives.

The act to issue the stock in payment for the territory, which became known as the Louisiana stock, was approved November 10, 1803 (2 Statutes, 245). It provided that, for the purpose of carrying into effect the convention of April 30, 1803, the Secretary of the Treasury should issue, in favor of the French republic or its assignees, certificates of stock for the sum of $11,250,000, bearing an interest of six per cent. per annum from the time at which possession of Louisiana might be obtained in conformity with the treaty, the certificates to be delivered by the President to the government of France, or to such persons as should be authorized to receive them, within three months after Louisiana should be taken in the name of the government of the United States.

The faith of the United States was pledged for the payment of the interest and the reimbursement of the principal, in conformity with the provisions of the convention with France.

The convention provided that the interest should be payable half-yearly, in London, Amsterdam, or Paris, and that the stock should be reimbursed in annual payments of not less than three millions each, the first payment to commence fifteen years after the exchange of ratifications. The act, however, provided that the Secretary of the Treasury might consent to the discharge the stock in four equal annual installments, and also to shorten the time fixed by the convention for commencing reimbursement. The annual interest, payable in Europe, was to be paid at the rate of four shillings and sixpence sterling for each dollar payable in London and two and a half guilders for each dollar payable in Amsterdam. Sufficient money to pay the interest for the first year was appropriated by the act. An annual sum of $700,000 (in addition to the annual sinking fund of $7,300,000), payable out of the duties on merchandise and tonnage, was appropriated, to continue so appropriated until the whole debt of the United States, including the stock created by the act, was paid.

Under this act stock for the portion of the purchase-money due France, amounting to $11,250,000, was issued. Its redemption began in 1812 and was completed in 1823, every dollar being paid. For the portion reserved to pay American citizens for spoliation ($3,750,000, no stock was issued, but the claims were paid in money, except the sum of $11,731.02 carried to the surplus fund June 30, 1868.

LOUISIANA SIX PER CENT. STOCK.

The act of November 10, 1803 (2 Statutes, 245), authorized the issue of certificates of stock to the amount of $11,250,000, the same to be paid over to the French government, in conformity with the provisions of the treaty of April 30, 1803, by which Louisiana was ceded to the United States. The reimbursement of the principal and payment of the interest were charged upon the commissioners of the sinking fund. No special revenues were appropriated or charged for the reimbursement. The stock was made reimbursable in four equal annual installments, and the rate of interest fixed at 6 per cent. per annum. The certificates of stock were made transferable only on the books of the Treasury Department.

Length of loan, 15 years; redeemable, in four equal annual installments, in 1818, '19, '20, '21; amount authorized, $11,250,000; amount issued, $11,250,000; sold at par; interest, 6 per cent., payable quarterly; final redemption, October 23, 1823.

ISSUES.

Calendar year.	First quarter.	Second quarter.	Third quarter.	Fourth quarter.	Total.
1804	$11,250,000 00				$11,250,000 00
Total					11,250,000 00

REDEMPTIONS.

Calendar year.	First quarter.	Second quarter.	Third quarter.	Fourth quarter.	Total.
1812			$322,500 00	$84,700 00	$[illegible]
1813	$[illegible] 00				[illegible]
1817		$14,000 00	$[illegible],000 00		[illegible]
1818	178,500 00	127,300 00		[illegible]	[illegible]
1819	144,000 00	[illegible]	[illegible]	[illegible]	[illegible]
1820	190,015 50	[illegible]	204,250 00	[illegible]	[illegible]
1821	[illegible] 50	2,071,152 00		[illegible] 00	[illegible]
1822			5,250 00		5,250 00
1823				2,500 00	[illegible]
Total					11,250,000 00

CHAPTER FIVE

DR. G. W. BOSTON'S CHART

Information regarding the chart he secured from Tuck Richards, and which Dr. Boston claims his wife burned by mistake with a lot of old papers while cleaning out his desk. That is what he told G.R.C. and has told other people.

He has also said that the chart is so worn that it cannot be deciphered. (take your choice).

Following is a description of instructions in the chart as given G.R.C. by Mr. David W. Gillett, father-in-law of Dr. Boston.

"Mound should be about four acres and should be on a South side. Measure——- chains N. E. and then ——— links North from foot of mound, across a ravine, and it is at once across the ravine."

Another time he said to G.R.C.: "It is in a mound place, a certain number of chains (number unknown) N. E. from foot of mound, to creek, thence a certain number of links (unknown) about North across the creek."

Dr. Boston told G.R.C. at Wauchula, Fla., May 8th, 1909 as follows:

"Beginning at landing and measure from there Northeast about seventy five steps of one yard each to a point (object unknown), thence more Northerly about twenty five or thirty steps to the left of a mound, evidently at the foot of it, in the hollow. Is in copper kegs."

Following is a copy of a drawing Dr. Boston made from memory and gave G.R.C.

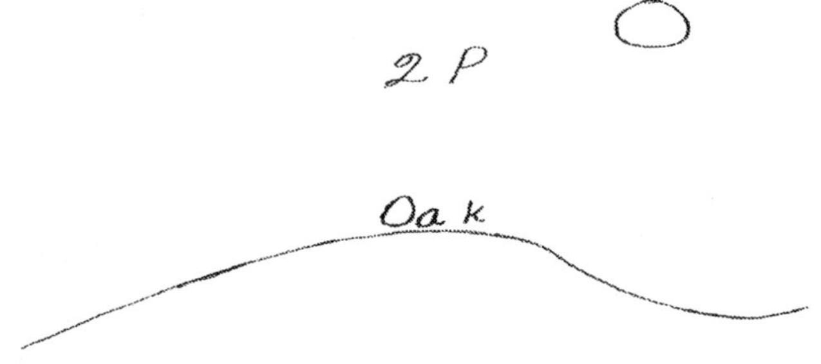

Dr. Boston and Mr. Gillett have hunted for that mound always but never could find it. Mr. O.H. Parker believed it was his "hammock mound" that was meant, but would never take either of them there as he

felt that he could not trust them to play fair with him as he always believed Dr. Boston did not lose the chart and thought they should produce it for his inspection. They, in 1909, thought "Johnson's Mound" was the right place, but the could not figure it out as the landing place was not right, but in 1919 G.R.C. found a very old landing place on a different point on that mound, all grown up with mangroves as to be completely hidden, and that may have been the desired landing place. It is quite sure that Mr. Parker never did test out these directions on his mound as it is doubtful if he went there after these directions were obtained by G.R.C., who showed them to him, but Mr. Parker made no copy of them. He used to ignore information unless it suited him.

By G.R.C.: There is a key of about 4 acres, all mound, in Turtle Bay, on South Side, which has never been examined. It should be and is the size Mr. Gillett says the Boston chart calls for.

DR. KELLY, GAINSVILLE, FLA.

Mr. O. H. Parker said that Dr. Kelly of Gainsville has a chart of a deposit in the water, which his father got from a patient, and that Dr. Kelly said he intended to come to Charlotte Harbor and search for it sometime.

May 17, 1919

(Supposed to be in Coral Creek, or at least the creek has something to do with it.)

Les working the coat hangers

CHAPTER SIX

GASPARILLA'S JEWELRY VAULT

In latter years Mr. O.H. Parker thought that information he got that the saw grass pond which contained the jewelry was to one in the forks of Coral Creek, as per the following diagram, but never got a chance to test the idea.

The statement regarding the jewelry is that it is in the middle of a saw grass pond, where the rocks are about four feet down, and it is in a large box (copper supposed) and can be reached in the dryest season of the year as the pond is infested with

moccasins. Can be gone into in June when it is dry. It is further said they carried in a large pine log, so large that it took about thirty men to handle it, and that they cut axe marks on it. That was the only mark by which to find the box. There is exactly such a pond, with a log in it exactly as described, and with three axe marks well toward the top which had to be made when the log was down on the ground, and the log is undoubtedly very old. That place is about four miles above the mouth of Coral Creek, opposite the cut-off and about a half mile from it. See diagram below.

Considerable digging of holes has been done around the edge of the pond by parties unknown, but there has been so much of it done that it plainly appears that those who did it had no definite instructions. There is one story that the appearance of a new moon shaped formation at the end of the pond, designated the pond. This pond has exactly that formation at its North end.

house
Gulf
island
cut-off
Pond
Coral Creek

About a quarter of a mile South of the pond, near the road to Englewood and about fifty yards West of the road, is a very large pine tree with the most elaborate markings and carvings on it that can be imagined, probably the most elaborately marked tree of the entire territory, and undoubtedly a hundred years old. The tree should be preserved but the lumber men will get it.

JEWEL POND

I made a flight down to the area specified in the "Papers" to see if a pond in the shape of a crescent could be seen from the air. There are a number of ponds in this area and there was one that almost exactly fit the description of the pond called for in the "Papers". From the air you can get a pretty good prospective as to the lay of the land and then when reviewing the topo chart you can see elevations that are not discernible from the air. The pond in question was fairly easy to get to as there was a trail off of a road that comes off the Placida / Englewood road and passes about 100 feet North of the pond.

A trip was planned and the four of us headed off for more riches. We did not believe that compared to the other "Tx's" that there would be much interest in the Jewel Pond. We just drove down to the trail to where on the Topo it appeared the best way to reach the pond by foot and walked right out to it. On arriving at the pond we discovered it was dry and a fire had been through it and made searching much easier. The search for the only mark called for in the "Papers", the pine tree, was begun and in the entire pond only one log was found. It did appear possible that this was the log called for as it did seem to be old enough and it was on the West side and was about the right size. There were no longer marks visible at the top as someone had tried to cover what marks that were supposed to have been there, by chopping through the tree close to the top. If this the log that was carried in by the crew, then parties unknown have tried to deface it or possibly tried to move it. We ran the machine at the top of the log where the copper box was supposedly dropped and got no indications of anything being there. I also worked the machine at every place where the copper box could have been relative to the log and got no indications. I believe that if Gaspar really had a different place for a TX that was only jewels, the settings probably were either sold as is or melted down for their gold or silver content and all that was in the copper box was jewels.

We did find indications that people were still coming to look for something around this pond, as we could see small holes dug around the edge. I ran the detector all along the edge of the pond where the parties unknown had dug the holes and got no indications of anything in the ground. These holes were too small to have contained something as large as even a small chest. This pond is not much of a pond anymore as there is now a drainage ditch now dug at it's South end and water no longer stands in it. The pond does have a extensive growth of Cat Tails but the fire had burned them nearly to the ground. Knowing that the cat tails would regrow as soon as a little rain fell, we determined that a trip in the very near future was necessary. We did spend the better part of the day surveying the situation, taking bearings on trees and other marks to exactly place the tree and trying to determine the best way to make a thorough search of this pond on our next trip as it appeared that we must not have interpreted the "Papers" correctly.

Our next trip had us prepared to do some serious exploring but upon arriving at the pond found the water to be 6 to 8 inches deep and that the Cat Tails had recovered from the fire sooner than expected and were now nearly 6 feet tall and very dense. With the pond and the surrounding area crawling with rattlesnakes and moccasins we decided to pull out of there for this day.

On days when things did not go too well or was very hot we had a "watering hole" in Oneco called the "Silver Dollar" and on more than one trip we frequented this establishment to discuss the events of the day, as we did when we believed that the jewels were already gone, or to drown our sorrows for once again coming home empty handed or just discuss how we were going to get our hands on all this wealth.

We made numerous trips down to the Jewel Pond and other than the first trip, something has always stood in the way of getting back to the pond and on the last trip found the property closed and No Trespassing signs put up.

We have also spent time looking for the large pine that was South of the pond and West of the road and it appears that G.R.C. was right, the lumbermen must have got it, as it is now gone. This tree could also have been a mark for the TX that was buried off of the cut-off at Cape Haze. It would be probably on the 67 ½ degree line run by G.R.C. and at its east end. This tree could also be a master mark for both of the treasures, the one at the Jewel Pond and the other off of the Cut-off, although this tree is not mentioned in any of the descriptions other than the mention by G.R.C. in this chapter.

Needing more information to further our research, we were led back to Squire's place which was now in a more comfortable home and on the corner where we turn to get to the "Jewel Pond". We found out that Ella knew also of the story of the Jewel Pond as well as we did. She said that it was her belief and that of other old-timers in the area that the Grandparents of a local resident who was connected with the bridge, that was privately owned, that went to Boca Grande, had found the jewels, as all of a sudden they had a lot of jewels deposited in a local bank. Now keeping something secret, as someone depositing a lot of jewels in a local bank in those days, was probably impossible. The Grandparents were said to be Spanish and possibly moved here for the specific reason to find the jewels and may have had information on exactly where to look. It is said that there is a woman in Cape Haze who is was writing a history of this family but as of the date June 1962, when this information was received, the book was not completed.

With this information that the jewels had probably already been found, we now believed that the log probably was the right one and the reason there were no indications is that there was nothing left to be indicated. The copper box that contained the jewels was gone and so there was no reason for us to return to the pond.

This was though, it appeared, another testimonial for the quality of the information contained in the "Papers".

Jewel Pond in 1959

CAPE HAZE

Just about due West of the Jewel Pond and across the road, is another location mentioned in the "Papers". This is the place where Gomez took Tuck Richards and was afraid to show Old Joe Anderson.

We made our first trip to Cape Haze in February 1960 and it was one of those very cold and windy days that every now and then does happen in Florida. One nice thing about hunting TX's when the weather is like that, it keeps the mosquitos away. This area was very easy to get to, you just enter the "Cape Haze Subdivision" turn North until you reach the large row of Australian Pines, park the vehicle and walk through the pines and you are there. It appeared that no one cared as to what we were up to as no one ever asked, or so much as said hello.

There were many areas of open space with only short weeds and scrubby palmettos, maybe 100 yards North was heavier growth and seemed to grow right up to the row of blazed trees. We could see the blazes easily from the South side but at one tree we did have to clear away the growth to see the mark. Using the directions in the "Papers" we searched for the sword grass pond and paced 100 yards East from each of the blazed trees. We did find what could be considered a sword grass pond but by this time there were no alligators living here. The pond was not too far West of the road. On this, our first trip, we were satisfied that it was worth a return trip.

Another trip was not made to the area until July 1960 and by then was really hot. We went through the same process of identifying all of our marked trees along with the tree with the long high blaze on the side toward the water that G.R.C. said that been cut down and was gone, but we found the tree just where it was supposed to be. The growth now was really thick. We began our search using the detectors and worked areas around 40 feet from the marked trees mainly to the East. After a couple of hours of the heat it was time for a break. We selected a small clearing that had no shade and only one very long dead pine tree.

After relaxing a few minutes and having something cool to drink, I walked to the dead pine an began to tap with a machete on what I thought was a knot and to my surprise the knot fell out and revealed what appeared to be chop marks. Now looking at the tree I could see another chop mark near the base of the tree. Walking around the tree I discovered another knot and tapped it in the same manner with the same result. This tree had three notches cut into it, two on one side and one in the middle on the other. This tree had to be very old, as all that was left was just about 6 inches diameter of the heart wood and was maybe 10 feet tall. It appears that someone deliberately had made an effort to disguise these chop marks and had done a real good job of it for as long as they have lasted. There is the story that Gasparilla did cut notches in his corner trees to use them as a mark. If the marks were made by Gasparilla and it was he who disguised them, he definitely is one sly Pirate. We left the area and expected to return soon but every time we got back in there it was very wet and could not do much.

We did return in May 1962, after a severe freeze. We were walking the marked tree line and when we reached the middle tree, the one which always had the most growth, we could see through the growth to the North was a very large hole that had never been visible to us before. This large hole was 40 feet North of the middle tree and was where it was called for as far as the 40 feet from a mark was concerned. The hole measured about 30 feet by 30 feet and was three feet deep with the bottom very even. This hole appears to have been dug by hand shovel and not mechanical means and quite a while ago as there was a palm tree growing out of one side of the hole that bent 90 degrees to the vertical. The detectors were run over the entire area, if just by chance something was missed, and got no readings. This site resembles a site that I saw on the St. Mary's River in North Florida where a group had excavated an area probably 4 times as large but about the same depth, where many ingots of something that appeared to be silver, even with the mint marks from the mint in Peru. A person I knew had gotten possession of a few of these ingots and they appeared to be the real thing. Even as you were led to believe that it was all silver it was not, although it did contain 6 % silver and many other metals that were included to make “bell metal” Where this find was made was at an old mission site and I guess the Indians ran them out before they could make many bells.

The “Papers” say that Old Joe Anderson’s sons are carrying the U.S. mail on this route to be able to stay near the TX. This writer tracked down both of Old Joe’s sons and spoke with both about this TX and both said that they did not know what their father was up to. If they were not telling the truth, they were hiding their wealth very well as one was working on a dredge out of Grove City and the other was still carrying the mail but now in Clearwater.

We did get a fairly good indication on one of our trips and was 100 feet East of the tree with the notches and this put it in the area of the sword grass pond. This is in the same area that G.R.C. mentioned in the “Paper’s” where they got “attraction”. G.R.C. and his people were using one of the earliest electronic metal detectors. We rodded down with the 7 foot probe and hit some resistence at 3 feet and were able to push through it and then we hit another spot at 6 feet and with a little more trouble got through it and to the limit of the probe rod. The area was so wet that we could not dig, so put off doing any thing that day since we knew where the spot was and we could find it again.

When we returned with the dryer weather we found that the notched tree was gone. Someone had cut a fire break with a bulldozer and had taken down the tree. A search revealed it in a pile of dirt pushed up by the dozer but a long way from where it belonged. The tree was our mark to begin our measurement of the 100 feet and now it was gone and the dozer had really messed up the lay of the land and now we had no idea where to start. We got discouraged and never looked anymore that day. This happened in June 1964 and for whatever reasons we never went back. This mark on the notched tree and the 100 feet East does fit some of the directions given in the "Papers" and just possibly is one of the many TXs that Gasparilla buried in the area. The hard layers that we hit could have been timbers laid in the hole after the TX was buried and over time rotted to where you could push a probe rod through them. According to the"Papers" one TX was 10 feet down and we only rodded to 7 feet. It would make sense to this writer that you could use the marks that you already had made for more than one TX. The large hole, dug not far from this location, could have given up some TX as I cannot see any reason for excavating such a large hole by hand for any better reason.

It is the opinion of this writer that if anybody had a good chance of recovering any of this it is probably old G.R.C. himself, he does mention doing a lot of looking, measuring and researching but never mentions putting a spade in the ground. Makes a fellow wonder

Corner tree with notches

1961
C&GS Chart 875B

"Colonel" at tree with high blaze

CHAPTER SEVEN

BULL KEY

CHARLOTTE HARBOR

This key is named after a Negro who was murdered and whose grave can be seen near the East end of the island (key) and close to the South shore of the island. Bull was the member of a fishing crew and got into an quarrel with another of the crew who stabbed Bull to death, and he was buried where he fell. Of course this name is recent, about 1890, and it is not known what the island's original name was.

From Oliver H. Parker, May 31st, 1919, though G.R.C. had heard the story many times before.

While Gasparilla lived here a vessel anchored a quarter of a mile South of Bull Key. They prepared to hide a lot of gold bullion. Gasparilla captured them, and they had about $6,000,000. He made every one of them walk the plank. One story is that they threw the bullion overboard to save it when *they saw Gasparilla's boats coming, another story is that they had it in their ship and Gasparilla sunk the ship, which is visible in low water at times, another story is they buried it on Bull Key, and still another story is that they buried it on Gasparilla Island, which is but a short distance West of Bull Key. The ship was anchored off the channel that runs South past the end of Bull Key.*

(West end I think).

Ideas of G.R.C.

They quite surely did not throw it overboard after they saw Gasparilla's boats coming after them because that much bullion would weigh twelve tons and it can hardly be supposed that they would have time to do so. By Gasparilla's "boats" it may be that his ships, of which he always had two or three, is meant, and it is a possibility that the ship of the strangers was so shot up in the fight that it shortly afterward sunk., and that is about the only way it would have been sunk for the crew most assuredly would not have sunk their own ship intentionally from under their own feet. The really strongest story and most persistent one is that it was buried on Bull Key, and most likely by the crew of the strange ship. It is said that this cargo of bullion had been captured by a part of the crew of a ship bringing it from Peru and after killing the Officers and all who opposed them they ran for Charlotte Harbor, which was known to an old pirate among them who did not know Gasparilla was in the vicinity.

BULL KEY

This island was the least searched of any of the islands in Charlotte Harbor, possibly due to the lack of any reliable information. Bull Key is just East of Cayo Pelau and is kind of long and narrow, running East/West. This island along some others in the area is owned or controlled by the Department of the Interior.

The history covered in the "Papers" would not give anyone a lot of confidence that even if they searched the entire island that much would be discovered. There is an island just to the East of "Bull Key" and it is named "Gallagher Key" and there is a "Gallagher" mentioned in the "Papers". There may be no connection but then again. We have never set foot on this island because we never had any real information about it and really do not have any idea when or why this island was named as it was, but if you happen to be in the area with your detector you might just stop by and see what you can find.

Our one and only trip was made in 1965 and two machines were used but they were the shallow depth variety and other than the standard junk usually found along the shore, nothing else was found. It is my belief that if what is said in the "Papers" is accurate, the Treasure was buried on Cayo Pelau. When you compare the two islands, I can't conceive why a Pirate would choose Bull Key over Cayo Pelau, given that they are so close together. I remember when I was flying over this part of Charlotte Harbor in the mid 50's that there was some kind of activity on the South end of Cayo Pelau. There was some kind of excavation and some equipment for digging. I am not sure of the amount of time, that whoever was there digging, but it seemed like a month or more. I remember asking what was going on and was told that Lowell Thomas (the famous radio broadcaster) was there looking for something. So, given the odds, I would guess that he had some good information and that it could have been what was mentioned in the "Papers". The treasures that I have heard mentioned relative to Cayo Pelau, all have been toward the North end, other than this one mentioned in the "Papers". Bull Key has no large trees but has a lot of Black Mangrove. We spent time looking for "Bull's" grave but there is nothing left to indicate that anyone is buried on the island.

The information in the "Papers" appears to be fairly accurate as to the water and channels that were around these islands. We made an attempt to search the water at the West end and South of the island to find any remains of the ship carrying the treasure. We went for a depth of 6 to 8 feet, a depth one would believe necessary for anchoring a vessel this size. The water on this day was very dirty and visibility was one foot or less, not too good with snorkles. The water here is not very deep and with a fairly decent underwater metal detector, I believe if there is anything left, it could easily be found and recovered.

We then went to Cayo Pelau to look at a cove that is on the East side that had caught our attention. There is a fairly deep channel that runs between the islands, that could easily handle a vessel of the size that was used by the pirates. When we entered the cove we shut down the motor and with an 8 foot pole attempted to pole our way around the cove.

To my surprise the pole would not reach bottom and upon trying to reach the bottom, I had to push my arm past the elbow just to touch it. The water depth was like this nearly to the edge of the mangroves that surround the cove. It is possible this cove was used by the pirates for keel hauling their ships to clean off the growth and re-caulk the bottom. The size of the cove appears to be plenty large and deep enough for this scenario to make sense. Just behind the mangroves and in the sand flat, I found a large cedar post that could have been used to attach a block and tackle for pulling from the top of the mast to pull the ship on its side.

If the ship mentioned in the "Papers" is where it says it is and was not a Merchantman, it probably had canon aboard. I do know of a group of canon that laid on a bar between the Myakka River and the

Peace River a mile or so offshore. Someone in this time period raised a lot of steel canon and they laid on the beach for quite a while on Pine Island near Bokeelia. I have no idea where in Charlotte Harbor they were found but could have been the ones between the rivers or maybe from the ship near Bull Key or some other place.

Pirates would try to have bronze canon on their ships rather than the steel ones for a number of reasons and the first is probably quite obvious, they don't rust. The other is that bronze can be shined to a degree and if they were being pursued by superior fire power, they could jettison the canon overboard and by losing the weight, they gain speed to out run the opposition and also they could head for shallower water, where the still armed vessel could not follow. When the engagement was over the pirate vessel would go back to where the canon were dumped and because they were shiny, were more easy to locate, recover and be back in business again. The canon could also be filled with treasure and the barrel plugs put in and jettisoned and recovered by the same process, for all the above reasons.

CAYO PELAU

There is no island on the West Coast of Florida with more lore attached to it than Cayo Pelau. I have heard of more treasures taken from this island than any other. If there were as many treasures found as I have heard of, then the ground would be just littered with doubloons and pieces-of-eight. We have given this island more than a cursory examination and I have heard people tell of treasures dug up from the same place we had just run our detectors and we had no indications at all and in my opinion these stories are no more than "balderdash". I know some of the people making these claims and I do have a real problem with believing anything said by them.

We never had any real information of where to look on Cayo Pelau but from the time we did spend on the island, we were able to find where the old artesian well was located but it is no longer flowing and probably hasn't for a long time. This well is probably one of the reasons that Cayo Pelau was popular with Pirates and others. There was still the evidence of the house of where Columbus C. McLeod lived and was killed, probably around 1920. Albert Lowd said that his father took the Sheriff to Cayo Pelau in his boat to investigate the killing of McLeod after someone had discovered him dead in his house. Albert's father said that there was so much blood splattered about the house that it looked like someone had chopped the head off of a turkey. Albert said that the Sheriff believed the killing was done by O. H. Parker but had no proof. According to the "Papers" this belief makes sense as they state that the two began to hate one another over a falling out over a treasure they believed to be buried off the island in the bay.

I have walked the West side of the island towards the North end and along that shore there is a lot of broken shells for maybe 100 feet. I found a large piece of clear green glass that came from a large (probably near 10 gallon) jar that is believed to have been made in the 1700's and came from France and had contained wine. I happened to go to a wine shop in Hartford, Connecticut when I was there on business in 1965 and saw the same colored glass on a large wine bottle and it was the owner who told me the probable date of manufacture and that bottles of this size were used in the wine trade. Some of this trade must have been in or near the Gulf of Mexico.

This is the same place that Parker and McLeod called "ballast point". I was lucky enough to find a small piece of malachite that was also on the beach. We did spend a lot of time looking for the pedestal, made of malachite, that supported the large flat rock covering the "TX" but never found a trace. Knowing that Squires had been in the area a long time it was a good idea to ask if he knew where the big flat rock was to be found. He said that he did know but would not tell us where, as it was covered with some of his favorite oysters and no matter how many promises we made to not disturb the oysters, he still would not tell.

If a person were to look around the north end of Cayo Pelau at a really low spring tide there is the possibility that they could discover where the big flat rock is and possibly it is in that same area where the pedestal may be. We have never tried this but common sense would tell you that the deeper the water the harder it would be to move a large rock and to the south and the west the water does get deeper. We never really felt it was that important to find something that no longer marked where the treasure was and in the "Papers" they say that Parker and McLeod did move the stone and to put up misleading sign. The only real value would be to give validity to this treasure. Malachite does have some semi-precious stone value and that much could still be worth something.

We have spent some time looking over both Devil Fish Key and also Sandfly Key. There is evidence of some small Indian mounds on both and seems that the pot diggers had made some effort to find relics here. The holes that they left were mostly shallow and there was some broken pottery near the holes as you find in "kitchen middens" or sometimes near graves. I never did see any evidence, where there was digging, of any human bones. We did not discover any trees on either island which we thought could be old enough to date from the time of the pirate. There were stories that the pirates had used these islands as some kind of mark but it is unknown whether the island itself was the mark or something else was the mark. If it was the latter, we were never able to discover it.

The story of Lowell Thomas having been on the island treasure hunting could be true, as we did explore the South end of the island where a mound of some size had been, and is now flat. I remember that what appeared to be a mound was visible on this end when I looked down while flying over Cayo Pelau in the mid 50's and now is no longer there.

This mound is where McLeod's house stood and has holes dug all over it, from the top of the island and mainly on the West side. There once was an artesian well, which has been dry for many years, mid island on the west side and this is probably why this island was or could be important. There were many artesian wells on the mainland but few islands could claim a well. There was a very large well or spring just off "Burnt Store" road near the shore and close to where the "Burnt Store" marina is today.

To me the most interesting parts of the island are to the Northeast and to the East towards the deep water cove on the East side. There is quite a bit of sand flat Northeast to East of the mound. When we were there last there had been little digging on this side. From the time of the Indians until when we were on the island there seems to have been a lot of human activity on Cayo Pelau.

Now if there is anything left on this island, in my opinion it is from the center of the mound towards the East side or in the sand flat. This is close to the cove that is mentioned in the part that covers Bull Key.

The treasure purportedly in the bay that was searched for by Parker and McLeod would require a detector larger than anything I could, at the time, afford and the retrieval would be something else.

My opinion probably agrees with GRC in that, the stone was probably only put there as a mark. If it was placed there as a mark and being as elaborate as it supposedly appeared probably was a mark for more than just one treasure. If that is the case, then this mark probably belongs to some other Pirate than "Gaspar" as the "Papers" never mention any thing about a mark such as this. That does not preclude the thought that the information that G.R.C. got was not complete. I don't think any Pirate would want to bury a treasure like this and then come back and go to that much trouble to retrieve his money. It probably took less effort to get it in the first place than the effort to try to hide it 30 feet down under the ground and under 3-4 feet of water.

This being said, there is the "Oak Island Treasure" that was put away much more elaborately than this and is what appears to be a engineering masterpiece. If the reader of this book has not read anything concerning the “Oak Island Treasure”, they should, as it is one of the greatest treasure mysteries that has not been entirely solved. So there is always the possibility that the mark at Cayo Pelau is really to show exactly where a treasure is buried.

1947 C&GS Topographic Chart

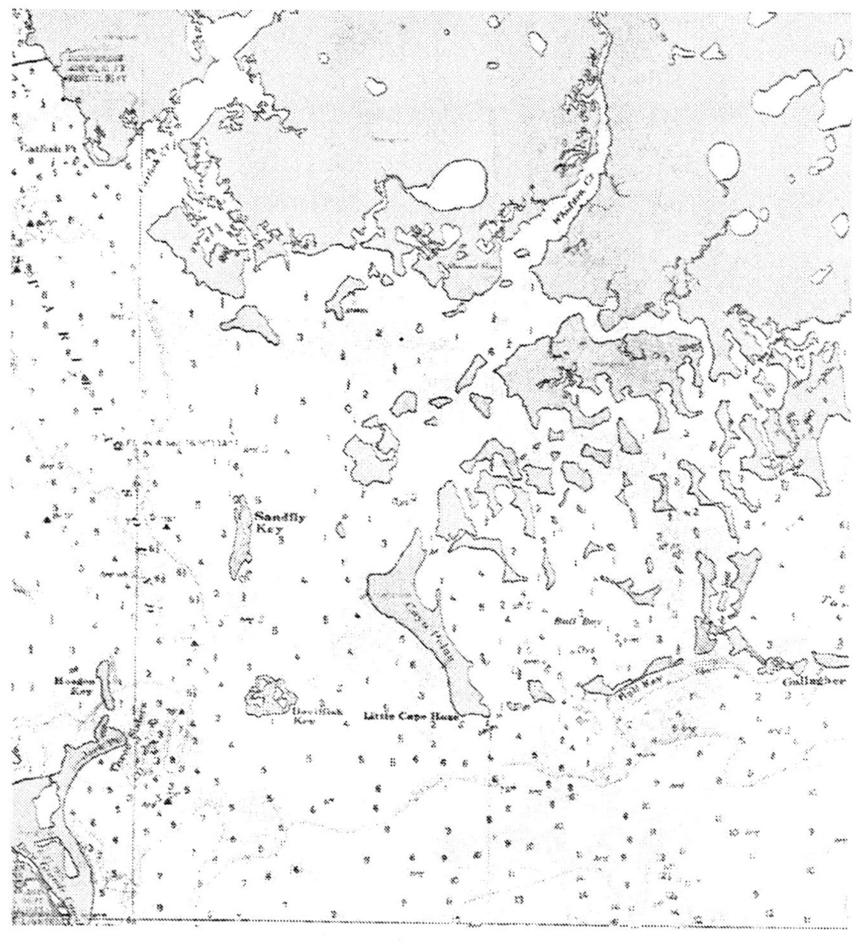

CHAPTER EIGHT

BAKER'S TREASURE ON LEMON BAY

O. H. Parker May 22, 1919

About 1822, Baker, who had been a very notorious pirate for a long time was preparing to quit piracy as it was becoming a hazardous proposition since the United States had bought Florida and had already captured a lot of their vessels and hung the crews and at that time his crew had dwindled down to about twenty five men as they had lost men in fights with vessels they had captured. One ship in particular put up such a hard fight that the Baker crew were nearly whipped and lost more than half their men before they won and they found little on the ship that was of value to them, so they decided to stop and divide their booty at which time amounted to about $3,000,000. Baker got information that there was a lot of U. S. Navy vessels in the Gulf and he was afraid to have his loot on his vessel as he feared the U. S. vessels would overhaul him and it would be his death *warrant if they found it. He anchored in the Gulf off the beach at the North end of Lemon Bay and took the money and put among the rocks East of the shore of the bay, about a mile South of its North end. As they were returning to their vessel they saw a U. S. vessel close by and headed for their vessel. They held a quick consultation and decided that there was nothing incriminating on board they could pass off as an ordinary ship's crew and all went aboard except two of the sailors (one named Harris) who were afraid to go. The war vessels officers boarded their vessel and examined them and the Captain (Baker), so it was afterward learned, told what he thought was a plausible story, but the Navy Officer told Baker that he had a description of him and knew he was Baker and that they had been searching for him and his ship. They hanged Baker and all his men and sunk his ship where she was anchored.*

Harris and the other sailor stayed hid in the brush and saw the hangings and got away in the brush and made their way to Pensacola and thence to Georgia. Harris

lived in Georgia many years and the other sailor stayed with him and died there. After the other sailor had died in about 1874, Harris decided he could come back to the place where they had buried the money without danger to himself but it was a harder task for an old man than he thought, and was so weak that he gave out before he could get there, though he nearly made it. He was found in the woods by Mr. Lewis Murray and Judge W. E. Loper of Grove City who were hunting. When they came upon Harris he was down on the ground and groaning and his groans attracted their attention. When they got to him he pointed for them to "go over the hill" and tried to talk to them, evidently thinking he was dying. They paid no attention to that at the time but gave him whiskey and coffee and got him to Judge Loper's house. He revived sufficiently to talk to them and thinking he was dying told them the whole story and tried to describe the exact spot to them and told them all he could. He lived a few days but did not get enough strength to be taken to show them where the treasure was put.

He said it was put among the rocks, did not seem to want them to understand that they had done other than hide it under the rocks and there is a rock formation there of not very large extent.

He died and they buried him in the new cemetery at Grove City and being the first man buried in it the cemetery is and always been called "Harris Cemetery".

The coils ought to find that with little difficulty.

1944
War Department
Corps of Engineers, U.S. Army

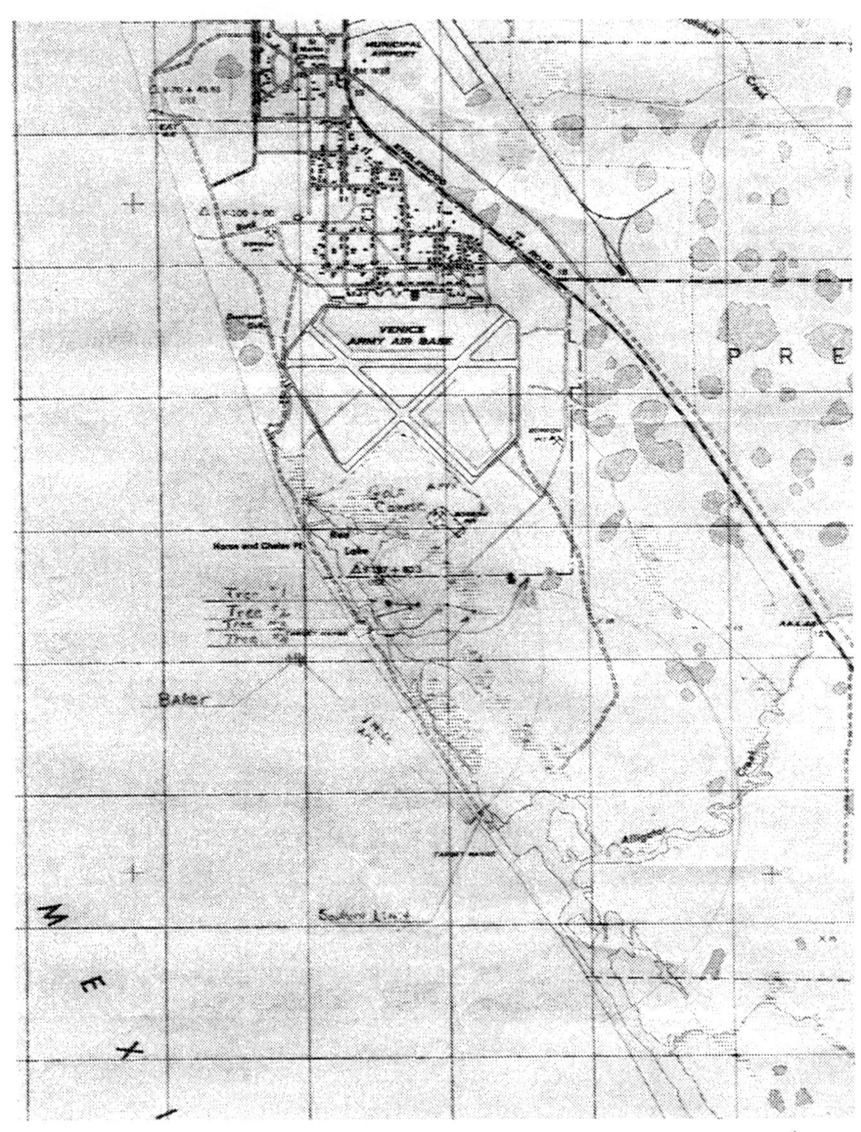

BAKER'S TREASURE

The "Colonel" had hunted a "TX" in this area from about 1950. He was involved with this group which was very serious about their treasure hunting. One of the group was William DeMoy, from whom the "Colonel" was given the "Papers" by Mr. Demoy's wife after his passing. I am not acquainted with any of his group other than the "Colonel" himself. I don't believe this group hunted any treasure other than this one. One of the people involved with this hunt either owned the land where they were searching or knew the owner.

The "Colonel" and his group had gotten a good indication from the "Colonel's" M-Scope in one area and proceeded to try to probe down to it with a 7 foot probe rod. Whatever was there was deeper than 7 feet. A decision was made to bring in a dragline with a clam bucket, pump to keep the water out and lumber to shore up the hole. They began the dig and continued down until they dug up parts of a skeleton and some wood at 16 feet. The "Colonel" decided it was a good idea to ride the bucket down into the hole and get close to whatever else was there. As he reached the bottom he was aware that there was a very strong odor of chlorine gas and made it known that he wanted out of the hole as quick as possible for his safety. He said that they wanted no longer to mess with this place and pulled out and never went back. I heard this story and wondered what could happen to cause the formation of that much chlorine gas. A little research turned up what appeared a plausible situation to cause it. When shells begin to decompose they can form both the acids, nitric and hydrochloric and if there is gold in this mix it will break down and form aqua regia (kingly water) and when it breaks down it makes chlorine gas. It is possible that something of value was in the hole but they say they never dug anymore to find out.

The description in the "Papers" does not really fit whatever the "Colonel" was on to and his group may have had different information than is contained in the "Papers" about the "Baker TX". One thing is for sure that an old man, by himself, could never have been able to retrieve whatever was in the hole. The description by "Harris" of the mark to look for was a "pile of stones" and there was never a pile of stones where they dug. It is on this premise that we decided to return to this area and look for what was indicated in the "Papers".

As soon as we reached the area, the "Colonel" showed us the hole they had dug and the marked trees that were a part of this exploration. It is clear that his group did dig a hole and that they did spend a lot of time and money in the process. It was plain to us that if we were ever to locate "Harris's" TX then we had to find the pile of rocks that marked the spot. There never was an attempt to work the detectors as until we were able to find a pile of rocks or anything that looked like where a pile of rocks had been, there was no need to operate the detectors. No rocks or a pile thereof was ever found. It does not seem to me that this area fits the description called for in the "Papers".

I believe that it is further South and where, just offshore, maybe 100 yards, are the remains of some old wreck and is just about where "Baker's ship would be, if it was sunk 1 mile South of the North end of Lemon Bay. This is where the land on the mainland side is somewhat higher, there is a creek nearby and it would appear, it could be easier to locate, if you were on a ship in the Gulf looking for some kind of mark for reference. There was no attempt to look in this area as development had started and never thought we stood a chance of finding anything. We came to this conclusion after being in and out of the area for 5 years. The area where we spent most of our time and where the "Colonel" made his dig, is now where the Venice bypass of the Inter-coastal Waterway enters Lemon Bay on the South side.

I have done considerable research looking for the cemetery that Harris was supposedly buried and called the "Harris" cemetery as he was the first person there. I have looked in Grove City and found no graveyard and have looked in Englewood at the cemetery there. There is no person named "Harris" that died in that time period with a marker. Being an unknown to the area, he probably was just buried and some kind of wooden marker was placed and by now wherever he was buried, the marker, is now long gone.

Head of Lemon Bay

“Colonel’s” Tree # 1

CHAPTER NINE
ODD SCRAPS

Following are odd scraps of information gathered by Mr. Parker from time to time and told by him to Mr. King.

Gomez said they cleared beaches at their place of rendezvous and made white beaches with shell. (Cayo Pelow is that way on the side toward Boca Grande Pass.)

Gasparilla always boasted after the pirate congress met that he could whip the American Navy.

Gomez told Tuck Richards that they put it where there were some little clumps or hillocks. Gomez told Richards that they made marks in zig zag. Parker says he and his brother James ran a lot of these lines and at the corner trees they would have lots of notches cut in them. I found shell mounds the same way. (King)

Gomez wanted to show Tuck Richards but he and his brothers kept putting Gomez off until they finished clearing some land. Gomez told them he was going to die, and they finally started out with the old man but after they got out a ways in the boat he became so sick they feared he would die before they could land. They went back home with him and he never recovered, died four days later.

Gomez told "Cap" Richards that there was a little pine growing near it, but that "it is dead now" always repeating this latter fact.

Gomez said he climbed up in the ship's rigging and "looked over" and saw them burying the TX.

Richards said there were six layouts of "it".

Mr. Parker asked Tuck Richards if they put it in the shell. Did Gasparilla put it in the shell? No, they put it in clean yellow sand. Put ship's ballast under it.

"Dr." (?) Richards said if we found any skeletons in a sand flat not to destroy them as they were the best evidence of the money, for they were close to it.

Gomez said it was buried behind two waves of the sea, made of shell and indicating waves with a motion of his hand.

They got the bullion in the latter part of 1818.

Gabe Marsh told James Parker that in a small pond 13 feet deep was a chest with a chain to it anchored to a tree and if he could find that he could find the money in a hour. Marsh is a Portuguese, last heard of in Tampa.

Capt. Roberts told Mr. Parker that Gasparilla broke up a lot of rock and scattered them along the beach for over 200 yards and used a lot of conks near TX. Parker asked "Is there any tree or mark near it?" Ans: "There is one little forked pine near it."

This conversation was in 1895.

CONVERSATIONS WITH MRS. COOPER-HOYE

Parker asked Mrs. Hoye did they put any jewelry in with the bullion? She said that Gomez said there were only one pair of fine bracelets and that he was going to get them for her. He said "I can't get it, its sunk, sunk way down.

Mrs. Hoye asked Gomez if they used any iron. He said "Yes they used lots of iron and that they put it in an open clean place."

Mrs. Hoye and her cousin Mr. Ellis says it is buried in an open sand flat in front of the biggest pass and where the tide water covers it. In an open clean place, no stumps, no trees, no marks, but there are palmetto trees around it, indicating by a wave of the hand.

Mr. Ellis was with "Bell" in the Seminole War, 1835 which lasted nearly eight years (war 1856 lasted two and one half years). Bell was mustered out in 1843. Bell said the money was buried 100 feet from waters edge.

Mrs. Hoye once said to Bell, "Mr. Bell I think that TX would sink. He studied a bit and said "I don't think it would, Mrs. Cooper, for we put it away right.

Bell said one day to Mrs. Hoye (Cooper), I got off one day from the surveyors and walked out on "it", "stamped over it", but to his surprise a little grass was growing on it.

"Robinson" told Mr. Parker it is in a sand flat where the tide water covers it, for Gomez told him so.

Old John Gomez, uncle of cabin boy Gomez, said they put it down deep in wells eight to ten feet deep, that it was covered with a big flat rock that took thirty men to lift.

Old Gomez said they put it down eight to ten feet deep to keep their own men from getting it.

They were routed by a Dutch Commodore in U.S. service in 1824. Gomez, the cabin boy, stolen by his uncle Gasparilla, was saved in the fight and Bell jumped overboard (Manitee River) and got off the other ship, neither knowing the other was alive.

Bell said it was put in a well eight feet deep and covered with a big flat rock.

E. S. Roberts told Mr. Parker they carried it one-eighth of a mile from where they landed it. Roberts and Robinson both said there was a little pine tree that had quite a bit to do with it (the TX) as it was not far from it. Roberts knows more about it as his father was a pirate and was hung with three others by the U.S. at Pensacola during the Civil War, about 1864.

(Note by G.R.C: From all the facts I think Roberts is talking of a different place than the one known of by Mrs. Hoye-Cooper, Selner and Bell. Bell seems to have known nothing of any of Gasparilla's TX except the Bullion, and Bell joined the pirates at the time that particular Bullion was captured in 1818 and was with them only six years. Capt. Roberts story to G.R.C. in 1919 does not in any particular apply to the Selner-Hoye proposition. It also seems that both Gomez's talked about the six different TX's, as they knew all of them and that is the reason for so many conflicting tales. Copied Feb. 1921.)

Memoranda, evidently from Panther Key (Cabin Boy) Gomez. "Blackbeard's treasure is on Blackbeard's Island, eighty miles from Savannah, Ga."

Statement made by Mr. David W. Gillett, Parisk, Fla.

(veteran of Seminole War, but not personal acquaintance of Bell) Casin

Cooper came with Bell and Bell walked out to a "litered" stump (a burned fire stump) and said "I am looking at it, meaning a TX. The Indians were beginning to get troublesome and they did not do anything. The next day the Indians killed two men named Hart and Owens. After the Seminole War Cooper moved to Little Manitee River.

Gomez the cabin boy died at Jack Leslies about 1889. Lived at Palmetto.

Gomez once showed two Spaniards named Dominic and Belota Lenarde, the latter a carpenter (Belota Lenarde) where there was a TX on Pepper Key at The Mouth of the Alipi River. These men were both poor men, yet one built himself a fine residence and lived easy, while the other bought a whole block in Tampa and also a dry goods store for his son. Mr. Gillett told me (G.R.C.) that these two men were old cronies of Gomez' for many years and had always played the old man so they believed they were true friends and maybe they were, but at any event, when he had gotten old and in poor health and thought that he could not live much longer and of course *having a good idea of what they wanted. He told them he knew of a treasure that contained between $125,000 and $150,000 and that if they would take a boat and go with him on Sunday, when they got off from their work, he would show them where they could get all the money that they would ever need, but with the distinct understanding that they would not disturb it until after they had taken him back to Tampa. They readily agreed to that and on Sunday took a little sail boat and the three of them went to the island, though Dominic and Lenarde had no idea where he was taking them and never suspected the island until he told them where to land. At the island he loafed around nearly all day as though reluctant to show them what he promised, but as it got towards evening he walked out to a very old oak tree and sat down in the shade and layed his hat on the ground a few feet from the tree, and after appearing to rest for a few minutes, Gomez got up, put on his hat and said "it's getting late, we better be going home again". Dominic and Lenarde hardly knew what to make of to make of it, but*

thought they understood what Gomez meant by laying his hat near the old tree and they had too good sense to ask questions or cross the old man, so they started for home, pulled out as they called it, and got back to Tampa about dark, or afterward. Not a word regarding the purpose of the trip had been mentioned by any of them all that day, but other things were talked about. In handling the situation that way it seems that Gomez was trying to avoid breaking an oath that he had taken, which all his uncle's men had to take, not to ever "tell or show" where a TX was placed, no other reason for his behavior can be understood, unless possibly a reluctance to part with the money himself and undoubtably he at the time was the only living man who knew of its location and he never at any time told its history. It appears that the next morning Dominic and Lenarde went there and alone dug where Gomez had thrown his hat and they found the TX just as expected and it was they who stated the amount, as Gomez never did say how much there was and seem never to have mentioned it except the one time he told

them he would show them where they could find all they would ever need.

Bell died at St. Marks about the close of the Civil War.

(Wrong, G.R.C.)

(Gillett still talking) TX lays on the North side of Coral Creek, 20 or 25 feet North of where Parker dug up Gasparilla's brother. The stump near it is burned to the ground and it stands between two cabbage trees. (Mr. Gillett showed G.R.C. the spot.) After the Civil War, Cooper and his family, Mr. Selner (Dutch) and his family came down here to look for it. When they landed Cooper said "we will get us a deer before we look for the TX". Picking up his gun he started around a clump of sword grass and Selner started around the other way. Cooper had gone but a few steps when he saw a deer and shot it and also two of the shot hit Selner. Leaving the deer laying on the ground he picked up Selner and carried him to the boat and hurried home. It came so near proving fatal to Selner that he will not venture near the TX again.

(This conversation between Mr. King and Mr. Gillett was just before Mr. Selner died at Gulf City.) Cooper made in all three trips to Coral Creek in his attempts to get the TX and eventually called it "three times and out ". Twice he was run out by Indians.

Mr. Gillett says one night he was laying with his head on a log and he dreamed the TX was just over behind it and this is the place he has also traced out as the correct place.

May 5th, 1909: Went to Placida with Mr. Gillett and went out in front of the store in the shade of some palmetto trees and Mr. Gillett told me I was standing over the "litered" stump, burned below the ground where he had located the place where the TX was.

Mr. Gillett showed us where old John Gomez, the cabin boy, took Tuck Richards and his brother-in-law and the brother-in-law Joe Anderson to show them where the TX was. While old Gomez was laying down supposed to be asleep, he heard Anderson (who was drunk) say, "he is asleep now, if Uncle John don't show us where that money is we'll kill him". This was on Sunday morning. Gomez was always afraid of Anderson. When he got up he walked away off and in an hour or so came back, walked out to a "litered" stump and leaned up against it and said, "I'm looking at the TX now, it's all there, turned and left them. He afterwards told Richards and his brother he wanted to show them the treasure but didn't want Anderson to be in on it as he was afraid Anderson would kill him. This place is nearly a mile from the entrance out of Gasparilla Bay into the cut-off that leads into Lemon Bay, is at the last bunch of Palmetto trees on the right, then walk across the old channel, dry at low tide, to a "litered" stump. Mr. Bell said it was a well marked tree and alive when he used to come to it. (It was alive in 1895 when G.R.C. first saw it, and marked with a long high blaze on the side toward the water and there were stones around the foot of it The tree was cut by fishermen about 1905.)

It died and was cut down for wood.

There is a row of blazed trees (blazeed on the off side) running 67 ½ degrees east to a

sword grass pond, about 100 yards is where they camped out and Gomez walked about 100 feet eastward and leaned against a stump. (This is all correct as to the row of blazed trees — G.R.C.)

By G.R.C.

This lead from Gomez is undoubtably one of the principal ones to his Uncle's TX for it was here that Gomez told and begged Frank Richards to come with him before he died and Frank Richards was hunting it at this place as late as the Spring of 1919. Bell never told the Cooper outfit anything about this location for he doubtless knew nothing of it as it must have been put there before Bell joined them in 1818. Bell seems not to have known anything about any TX except the Bullion which he himself helped put away at Coral Creek. Gomez would talk of the Bullion, but he never seemed to take any interest in it as it was not coined and he seems to have tried to lead his friends where there was coined money. In Gomez' talks about the bullion he would say "there was a mint of it" but never seems to have been interested in it.

Old Joe Anderson's two sons are now (May 5, 1909) carrying the U.S. mail between Placida and Englewood. (It is the presumption they are on that particular work to be where they can try to locate the TX but it is doubtful if they know anything of value to them.) Joe Anderson was a brother-in-law to Tuck Richards and Frank Anderson, as was Mr. Gillett.

Dr. Boston of Wauchula is a son-in-law of Mr. Gillett. Mrs. Boston is now dead.

(By G.R.C. One of Tuck Richards' sisters or daughters had a chart or map to the TX and DR. Boston being in the family got it from her and refused to return it and finally said it had been burned by mistake with some old papers. It is believed Boston still has that chart though it is of doubtful value. Dr. Boston described the ground called for in the chart and if he told the truth his description does not fit either the land around Coral Creek or the place where Gomez was when Anderson threatened to kill him, but applies to some high mound place, similar to where Gasparilla once lived on Johnson's Mound.)

P. T. Meharg

MAP OF PLACE AT PLACIDA POST OFFICE

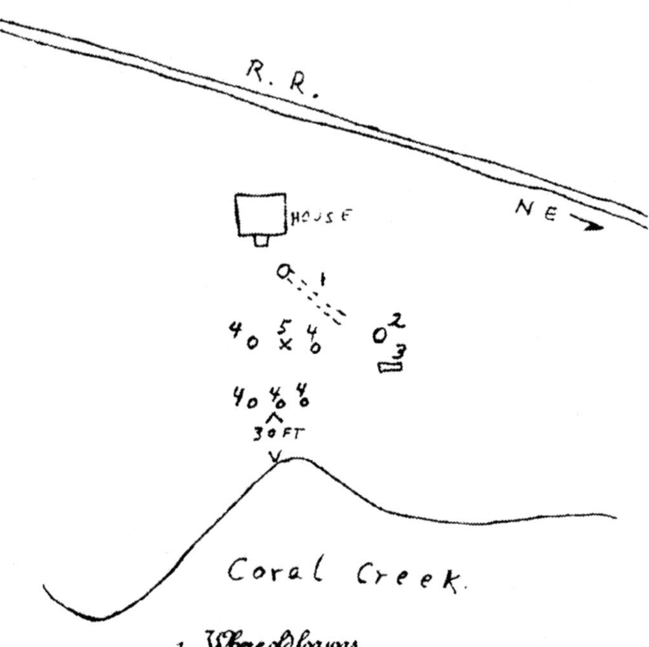

1. Where old log was.
2. Live oak
3. Where skeleton was dug up by Parker. Gasparilla's Brother
4. Palmetto Trees.
5. Where stump is, vault is supposed to be right North of it.

(30 feet from palmettos to creek)

TURTLE BAY

The search for the "TX" mentioned in the "Papers" about the Dr. Boston deposit led us to some very interesting places. We at first believed that it could be the Indian mound that we were already working at Coral Creek. Try as we may, the description could not be worked out at this location. In and around Gasparilla Bay there are many Indian mounds and any one of them could be the one called for, so we set out to examine any and all of the Indian mounds we could get to. I once again flew down and took pictures for our reference and also got the current topo chart to do all of the preliminary research before going to this area. By flying over these areas, one could determine the best way to get to them and places to secret the boat as to not attract too much attention. The two mounds in Turtle Bay looked interesting and one, possibly by coincidence, is called "Cash Mound" and the other called "John Quiet". Research revealed that Albert Lowd of Boca Grande knew the original names and that they were "Powder Horn Key" for the "Cash Mound and "Parkers Mound" for the "John Quiet" although he did not know the time or the reason for the name changes.

Our first trip to the "Cash Mound" was in August 1959 and upon landing, we observed what appeared to be a ravine right through the middle of the mound. This looked like the description called for in the "Papers", so the detectors were fired up and we began to search. This mound was not heavily grown over, so working the machines was relatively easy. As we searched we discovered that this mound was infested by the largest wasps that I have ever seen and seem to be nesting below the ground in the shells. To our good fortune, they were not aggressive so we continued the search.

Aerial Photo of Cash Mound in Turtle Bay

Much time was spent exploring this mound but to our disappointment, there were no indications on the mound. We did find a fairly large excavation on the East side of the mound measuring 6 feet deep and 6 feet by 8 feet wide and we machined around the area and got no indications there either. Along the shore we did find evidence of someone being on or around the mound. We found a wrench, some pieces of some engine and metal so encrusted, as to be impossible to determine what it was but for sure it was valueless. There is a small mound just North of the "Cash Mound" but we never spent much time looking at it although there was considerable digging of small holes on the mound, actually more than on the big mound. Just behind these mounds to the West is a large sand flat that continued on quite a ways towards the "Boggess Hole". We really believed that this could be the mound called for and decided the best thing to do before getting real crazy about it, was to discuss it with Albert Lowd to see if he knew anything about the ravine. The following week we made a trip to see Albert and found him at Squires house and he filled us in on the other part of the "Cash Mound" story. He said that the ravine was made by a steam shovel that was brought in to excavate shell fill for the original bridge between Port Charlotte and Punta Gorda. Before the workers started digging he said they found 12 palm log houses on the top of the mound and were supposed to be Gasparilla's. It is my guess that in the excavation process the men found some sort of "TX" and from then on the name of the mound was the "Cash Mound". If there is any truth to the story that the palm log houses were Gasparilla's, then the possibility of the original name of the mound was "Johnson's" and the sand flat to the West, and the small mound just to the Northwest, really should be explored. We made numerous trips to this mound in search of "crew money" and that is why, regardless how much we looked, we believe that the crew had found all there was to find. The Indian mounds of that time were not protected and were a cheap source of shell road material.

Next we came up with the idea that possibly the crew had stashed their part of the loot on the other side of Turtle Bay on the "John Quiet" so another series of trips were executed. The "John Quiet" is relatively clear of growth and appears that at sometime someone had lived on the mound. There were few trees of any size and many small holes dug by "pot hunters". There were parts of an old wood stove, many old broken bottles and many things that one would expect to find at an old homestead. Through the mangroves to the East of the mound is quite a large sand flat. I believe that on this little peninsula is the place where some surveyors discovered the remains of an fairly large vessel that they estimated was over 100 years old. If the boat was this old there is a good probability that it was a sailing vessel as there were only a few powered boats of any type (steam or gas) around Florida at that time. There was an article in the St.Pete Times in the early 60's that had covered this discovery. We were hunting this area at the same time and found where some surveying was being done and it is our guess that this was the area mentioned as the article just mentioned that it was in Charlotte Harbor. The old navigational charts do show that there is fairly deep water just East of the point, running from the point towards the Myakka River.

We did spend an adequate amount of time searching this mound and other than the standard household junk you would expect to find where someone had lived, that was it. We discovered an old trail leading due West from the large mound and where the trail meets Turtle Bay the beach was white with shell. These two mounds are owned by the Department of the Interior although they were not marked as they should have been.

We then decided that a trip to "Mound Key" was now called for and scheduled one when we were able to go. Ella Squires had said that she knew a man who had lived on "Mound Key" and had discovered a treasure where the mound had started to erode or wash away one day while walking around. As he was trying to recover it, he said he was attacked by ghosts trying to protect the treasure, so he quickly gave up the digging and never went back. Albert Lowd, Ella's brother, said that Mound key was once called "Dudley's Key". We did not put much stock in what the man had said about the treasure and the ghosts but the mound was in the area where all this pirate activity was going on, so just maybe it might fit with something that was in the "Papers". When we got to the mound it was mid summer and the mosquitos were awful and made this day most unpleasant. It was plain from the beginning that we definitely were not the first to look here. There were holes dug everywhere and some of them quite large. There were many large trees with marks on them but most have been cut into and it is now impossible to decipher what they said. You could tell that someone had also lived on this mound by the broken bottles, old pots, pieces of a wood stove and pieces of lumber. We worked the detectors in areas that we felt had some promise but found nothing. The rumor mill had it that a group from Sarasota and one from St. Pete were really hot on this mound and later one of these was supposedly arrested for trespass and because they had torn up the mound so badly with a bulldozer they were required to restore the mound close to its original condition due to the damage that they had done. This mound is supposedly owned by The Conservancy who also own "Mound Key" in Estero Bay.

Mound Key is near another site that offered some interest. The "Boggess Hole" is the site of the old Boggess homestead. Although there was no mention of this area in the "Papers" it is without a doubt a place that would have been known to any Pirate in the area. Having reviewed our topo chart, a trip was planned to get, by water, to the "Boggess Hole". Les and I, on this trip, took a small aluminum boat and upon arriving at Gamalama Key creek found that the tide was going out very rapidly and this small lightweight boat was just the thing to navigate fast running water in a creek with many sharp turns. As we progressed up the creek, mullet, as thick as I had ever seen them, were making their way to the bay. I was in the bow and using an oar to keep us out of the mangroves and told Les that the next big mullet that came by I was going to get him with the oar. As the next school came by the boat I selected a big one and caught him right behind the gills and stunned him real good. We cut the engine and drifted back to where he was and boated him. This mullet probably weighed 3 pounds easily. Les had him for supper that night.

Upon reaching the "Boggess Hole" all was quiet and the water 3-4 feet deep. On the North East side of the lagoon is the highest ground and is about 10 to 20 yards wide and maybe 100 yards long, wrapping somewhat around the lagoon. We landed the boat where there had, it appeared, been some kind of camp. This area was fairly narrow, so we kind of high spotted the area and due to some bad weather approaching looked as if would making our trip home in this small boat not much fun. So we departed "Boggess Hole" with every intention to return, which of course we have not done. This place, I feel still does hold some promise, if it is still the same as when we were there but probably has changed as much as the rest of this area. This place is a beautiful scene, reminiscent of how Florida at one time must have appeared to those who first ventured to these parts, a small peaceful lagoon, many fish abounding and birds of many species all around. This is just some of the pleasures of hunting the "TX" and if you are able to enjoy just being "there" then possibly you have found the real treasure.

TREASURE MAP
COPY OF ETCHED MAP ON PEWTER PLATE
SUPPOSEDLY FOUND AT SHELL CREEK
PUNTA GORDA, FLORIDA

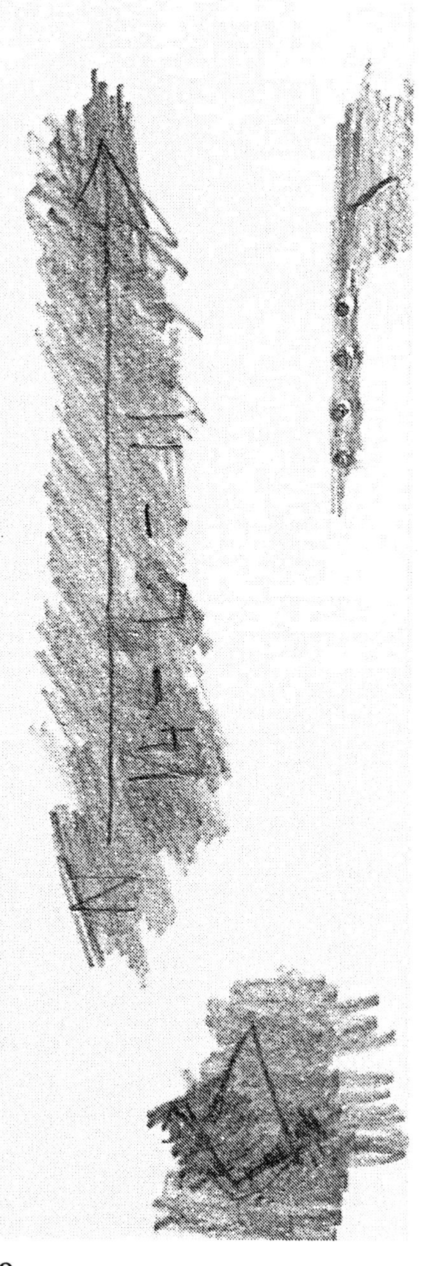

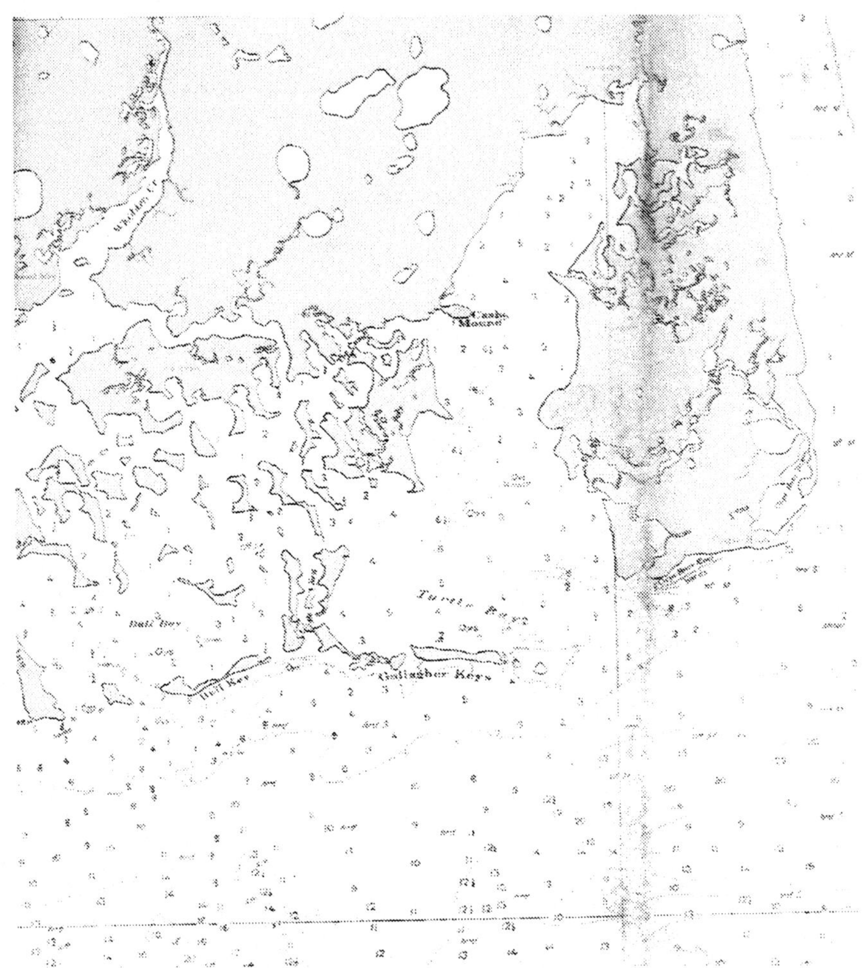

1947 C&GS Topographic Chart

CHAPTER TEN

GONZALEZ

Gonzalez purportedly was a small time pirate that operated in and around Charlotte Harbor and the Peace River. He supposedly had a warehouse somewhere up the Peace River. The following is an interpreted version of his directions to his or some ones treasure.

Locate O-X marking at Lettuce Lake - Travel N by W 1/4 W for 1800 feet. Examine area about 4 yards circumference. Locate O-X marking. Travel SW by W approximately 4 yards and examine area mark X.

It is any body's guess if this is authentic or not. There were so many people looking for treasure in or around the mound here and Lettuce Lake that this writer has never tried to find out.

GONZALES

MAP ON LEAD PLATE
COPIED FROM MEMORY

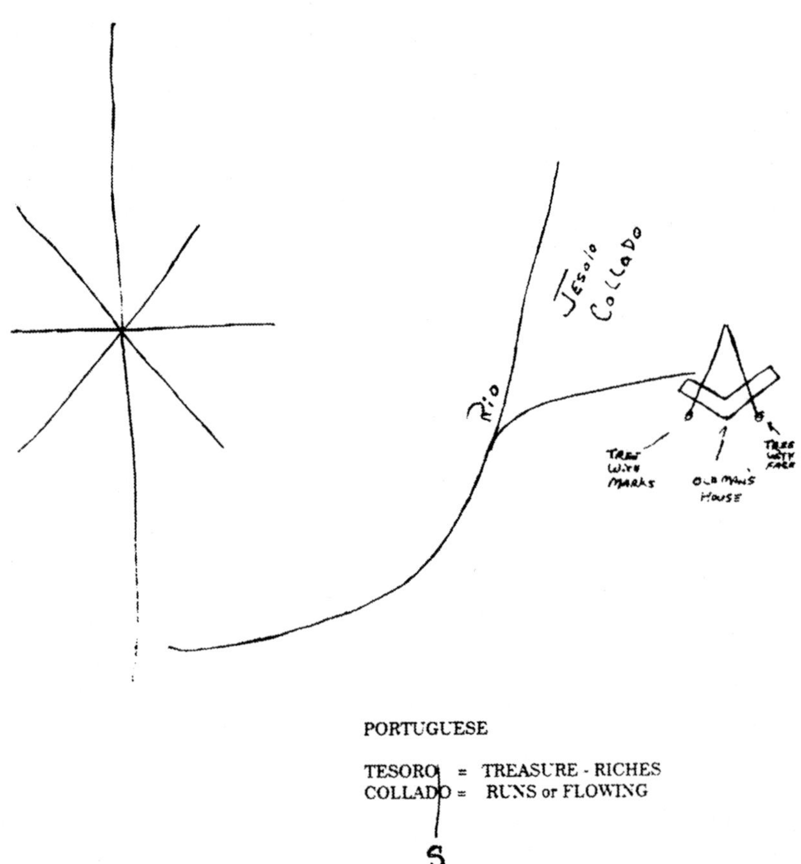

In 1966, probably close to one of my last expeditions, I went with a long time treasure hunter of questionable character, to look over an area he said was where Gonzales had hid some of his treasures. This place is about 1/3 mile downstream below the bridge (SR 781) where it crosses the Peace River and on the East side. The place is where the second tree leans out over the river. He said it was it this place where he found the pewter plate with markings on it, supposedly showing where the TX was buried. Frank said that as he had it figured, the TX was 40 degrees and 180 feet from where he found the plate. We spent most of the day clearing the area and working the detectors. It probably wouldn't surprise you if I mentioned we didn't find anything. This whole area has been dug over by Frank, the bunch out of Sarasota and probably many others. While we were here Frank told me that he was shown a place 1/4 mile further down river and on the East side where there had been a warehouse that was Gonzales's and that he sold goods to the settlers in the area. When leaving the first area we headed down river and at about where the warehouse was supposed to be, there was a clearing. I asked Frank to stop the boat so we could look over this spot to see if maybe there was some truth in this warehouse tale. Nothing doing, Frank was one of those hardheads who believed if it wasn't his idea, it was a bad idea. Needless to say this was my first and last trip with him.

A few weeks later Les, Bob and I went back to this area with some new information we wanted to check out. Instead of looking on the East side of the river the information suggested we should be looking on the West side. This information said the treasure was buried in the bottom or the side of a small ravine. We found a place where there was something, that if you stretch your imagination might be called a ravine, but it was where the information put it. This place was really gown over and we would have been there forever if we had decided to clear it. We decided to just kind of crawl our way up this place, going slow, on the lookout for snakes and working the machine. This ravine (ditch) appears to be natural and went up a small rise about 75 yards. Out of all this effort the only thing found was a old copper 10 guage shotgun shell.

There possibly at one time was a Pirate that made his hideout some where up the Peace River. The "Papers" never mention anything about anything buried here nor mention the name Gonzales, it could be that he came along after Gasparilla. The mound near Lettuce Lake supposedly was named "Parker's Mound" and could be connected to the Parkers mentioned in the "Papers". The last time I went by the mound it looked as if the City of Punta Gorda had built a water treatment plant on it.

CHAPTER ELEVEN

OTHER TREASURES

JEAN LAFITTE

The “Papers” do mention Jean Lafitte, where he had a small treasure buried and where his boat is sunk. This information only covers LaFitte’s second time on Florida’s West Coast.

Jean LaFitte had roamed the Gulf of Mexico and the Caribbean sometime in the years between the Battle of Trafalgar and the War of 1812. At the Battle of Trafalgar, in 1805, LaFitte supposedly had his life saved by Odet Phillippe, a person who it is said to have been a surgeon in Napoleon’s army. It is believed that sometime after the battle, for some reason, Phillippe was brought to the Indian mound at Safety Harbor on Tampa Bay (now called Phillippe Park) to set up a homestead to produce provisions for LaFitte’s ship (s). At the waters edge there was set up some type of still to boil salt water to get salt. For years there were pieces of fire brick to be found along the shore south of the mound. Inland was a farm and a grove of citrus.

Not far west from the mound was said to have been a monastery from the early Spanish period at which there was a well and that the monks or the

Spanish had dumped gold, silver and other artifacts to keep the Indians from getting them. I know of many treasure hunters who have searched for this well and some said that had found it in a pasture owned by the Booth's. None admitted to finding any gold or silver.

It is in this mound that LaFitte buried his largest cache. There has always been a small amount of information and rumor linking LaFitte to this Indian mound. Someone must have had some very good information based on articles that appeared in the St. Pete Times. The "Colonel" had both and they were in the Times in 1949 and 1950. The first article covered an agreement between the Pinellas County and three local individuals that an 50/50 split of a treasure to be taken from the Indian mound at Safety Harbor. The individuals that were named in the article but are not being exposed in this book but what they were will be. One was an attorney, one a state road department supervisor and an owner of a local warehouse. You will later see, why what they were is important. The second article covered the County's backing out of the agreement.

A longtime treasure hunter and friend said that in 1950 the three individuals (one an attorney, one a state road supervisor and one who owned a bonded warehouse) decided to retrieve the treasure anyway. The amazing thing, he said, was that state road department laborers were brought in and caused to dig the hole (actually in the side of the mound) until the timbers that blocked the entrance to the vault were exposed. The laborers were then dismissed and the three principals removed the timbers and exposed the treasure. It is said after loading a state road department truck with the treasure, they put the timbers back in front of the vault and left the area. They then brought back the laborers and refilled the excavation. One intriguing thing said by this group was, that they left all the "historical artifacts" in the vault.

There has long been a belief that Hernando DeSoto had been at this same Indian mound and is where they started their trek through the South. The diary kept by the Monk that accompanied DeSoto made mention that they had buried many things to keep them from the Indians as they had planned to return and get them. An Indian pot was dug up at the north end of the mound around 1948 by a St. Pete fireman who was also a treasure hunter, and that it had depicted on it, what appeared to be three vaults. Since the Indians that made the pot were long gone by the time LaFitte was here, there is the great possibility that DeSoto had made the vaults and the Indians made a record of it by putting what they saw on a pot, and somehow LaFitte had previous knowledge of the vaults or discovered them by accident.

The person who discovered the pot had some serious threats made to him about what would happen if he did not give up looking for the treasure. Another treasure hunting friend told of hunting this treasure in the early 1950's and would go there late in the evening so as not to be discovered. He surely was not aware that this treasure was already probably gone. The last time that he was there looking, he was found out by a sheriff's deputy patrolling the County property and had to run for it. He got in his car and with the deputy in pursuit, was chased over two counties by the sheriff's of both the counties. He said he finally was able to elude them but he said he has never made another trip to this mound.

I met a woman at a meeting of the Pinellas County Historical Society in Clearwater, who also was a believer in the probability that DeSoto had begun his march North from the Indian settlement north of Safety Harbor. The Smithsonian dug around this mound in the middle 1920's and is where the name The "Safety Harbor Period" was begun. I believe that in the book that was written by the Smithsonian about this dig, mentions Spanish contact with the Indians but does not mention DeSoto. This woman later showed me a silver candelabra and a dagger with a silver sheath, that she said were given to her by a Tampa Bay area attorney who stated they came from a mound on

Tampa Bay and that they had never been in contact with the soil. The antiquity of both items dated them to the 1500's, the right time for DeSoto and too early for LaFitte. It was her belief that the items were left behind by DeSoto.

There are the remains of a ship between the mound and the Booth Point in the deepest water. There are some rumors that a ship was attacked and sunk while she was at anchor in this area. It is also possible that it could be one of DeSoto's ships, as he left them wherever he started his march and only one returned to Spain. DeSoto probably left a small crew to tend the ships, expecting to return and return to Spain with gold and great stories for the Queen. It is a historical fact that he never returned. The crew that he left to tend the ships was too small to crew a flotilla but maybe enough for just one ship and I know of no history as to what happened to the rest of his ships. Every time that I planned a diving trip to this spot something came up and never got to explore the possibilities of either situation.

In the late 1950's the waters at this site were fairly clear as most dredging was being done in the South part of the bay. The best one could expect in those years would be between 3 and 5 feet. The 1879 Coast Chart # 177 shows 10 feet of water. This is an ideal depth for the anchorage of ships drawing the amount of water that they did in the 1500 to 1800's.

I spoke with a man who worked on a dredge that dredged the channel for the Booth Point Power Plant and that an large anchor had fouled the dredge bit and it had been retrieved. It was hit where a stern anchor would have been if either of these scenarios are accurate. He said it was a very old anchor and from its size probably a stern anchor. I don't know what ever became of it or if it had been dated by some expert.

It is this writers belief that of the research that he has done, most of all the things buried by DeSoto are still in the vaults awaiting discovery. With the new ground penetrating radar the area where the vaults are supposed to be could be examined with no damage to the areas at all. If the vaults are there then a controlled dig could be done by credentialed archaeologists and if there are artifacts from De Soto's time the county could possibly build a Museum at the site for all to enjoy and resolve the argument for all time exactly where DeSoto landed and started his march. I had an aunt who was born in 1903 in a small community on the shore of Tampa Bay close to where Allen's Creek meets the bay and by coincidence this community was called "DeSoto".

USEPPA ISLAND

The "Colonel" related to me, about when he was able to get on Useppa Island to work his detector. He said that the owner of the hotel end of the island had given him permission to examine the area with the machine but under no circumstances was he to dig or poke any holes in the ground. The "Colonel" said that he agreed to the terms and began looking over the island. He said that he had discovered a treasure buried on the island. It was, by the way he triangulated it with the detector, attached to a length of chain and the chain was connected to a canon. Pirates did bury treasure using this system at times. He told me that it was South of the hotel, just West of where there were some small steps leading down onto the golf course. This was sometime around 1956.

In 1961 we returned to Useppa hoping to get permission from the new owner to search and possibly retrieve this treasure. As we approached the dock on the West side of the island, a number of men dressed in army fatigues and carrying menacing looking weapons motioned for us to leave the area, which we did, post haste. Later we found out that these men were CIA and were training others for the "Bay of Pigs" invasion of Cuba.

Years later in 1978 I ran into a friend, Don Starr, who was then the Dockmaster at South Seas

Plantation, the latest owners of Useppa Island. I, related the "Colonel's" treasure story and asked Don if he could get me permission to search on the island. In April 1979 I got a letter from Don affirming that he had gotten me the ok of the owners. My large detector, a Fisher Super M-Scope, required new batteries and being and old machine there were no batteries for it locally. I was able to order some from Fisher and at the time they advised that these probably the last batteries ever to be had for the machine. This machine was no pleasure to work, especially when the weather was hot as it usually is in Florida, as it weighed 42 pounds and took both hands to carry but it was able to penetrate to a depth of about 22 feet. After satisfying myself both machines were working properly, I was ready.

I called Don and made arrangements to stay at South Sea's Plantation and he offered to transport me back and forth to Useppa in the company boat, as the owners were now going to share in the treasure I was sure to dig up. Upon arriving at the island I made my way to the area the "Colonel" described and without much trouble located where the steps were located. I fired up the machine and was ready to find the treasure the "Colonel" believed he had discovered. Soon the machine was making the desired sounds and I selected the one that most sounded like a box. Without the same restrictions as placed on the "Colonel", I began to dig and in short order found my treasure, a brass "Rain Bird" in excellent condition. The "chain" turned out to be a length of 1 inch galvanized pipe and the "canon" was a piece of 4 inch pipe. All of this, was at one time, used to irrigate the golf course that was available for guests of the old hotel. The "Colonel's" machine did as good as it could, it gave indications of something buried and the Rain Bird tended to scatter signal and made itself appear bigger than it was. Too bad the "Colonel" did not get to dig as he would have had the same result as I.

I spent two days looking all over the island, on any place that did not have a house and still did not produce much of anything.

I also spent time working the detectors near where there had been a flowing well at one time and where a treasure was purportedly found, but got no indications there either.

Thanks to Don, Dean and Gar Becksted, I am satisfied there is nothing left buried on Useppa Island.

SOUTH SEAS PLANTATION

Captiva Island, Florida 33924 • Phone (813) 472-5111

April 4, 1979

Dear Phil:

No, I hadn't forgotten our conversation last December about the treasure of Useppa Island.

In fact, it's taken me this long to get the OK from the owners to let you come on the property and do some digging. You'll have to be pretty convincing as others have come through the place and left nothing but a bunch of holes in their wake. They don't want that to happen again, and they're being very selective on granting permission to certain individuals.

I'm certain the owner will want to share to some degree in whatever you may come up with, and this you'll have to work out for yourself.

Let me know when you plan to come down and I'll do what I can to assist you from this end.

Also, can you send me some info on prices at Grand Cayman? I'm thinking about taking the family there this summer for vacation, so I'll need some brochures with prices, etc. Perhaps Mr. Tibbetts could be of some help?

Thanks, and stay in touch.

Tight lines,

Don

MEMBER: DISTINGUISHED HOTELS OF THE WORLD

THE HOUSE OF THE ADMIRAL

There is some doubt to whom this Treasure is attributed as I have never heard of it being connected to Gasparilla. Because of this treasure map there have been many people who have hunted for what ever was buried and it may well have been the small treasure taken from Useppa Island as it was taken close to the line that would be run from the Admiral's house to the Pine. The Treasure supposedly taken from Mondongo Island could also make it the one.

The "House of The Admiral" was purported to have been located on the highest Indian mound on an island in Charlotte Harbor. Where the hotel is located on Useppa Island appears to be the highest point of that island. Patricia Island just to the North seems just as high and it is also possible that Mondongo to the North West of Useppa, as Mondongo at some time did have a large Indian mound.

In the tales of "Gasparilla" there is a tall pine tree that is referred to as the "Lookout Pine" but is supposed to be on Gasparilla Island near Boca Grande and not on Cayo Costa where the "Solitary Pine" is shown.

Of the many people who have hunted this TX, I know of just two who spent much time at it. I have only made one trip to discover where the "Solitary Pine" stood. Les, my son Bob and I made a two day trip to the island, camping out in Les's boat on a sand bar just to the West of Cayo Costa. We spent most of our time trying to locate anything that would indicate that there was or had been a tree that would fit what the map called for. There were "solitary pines" and also some in groups, nothing to make one believe that he had located the "Solitary Pine".

TREASURE MAP OF AREA AT
BOCA GRANDE PASS

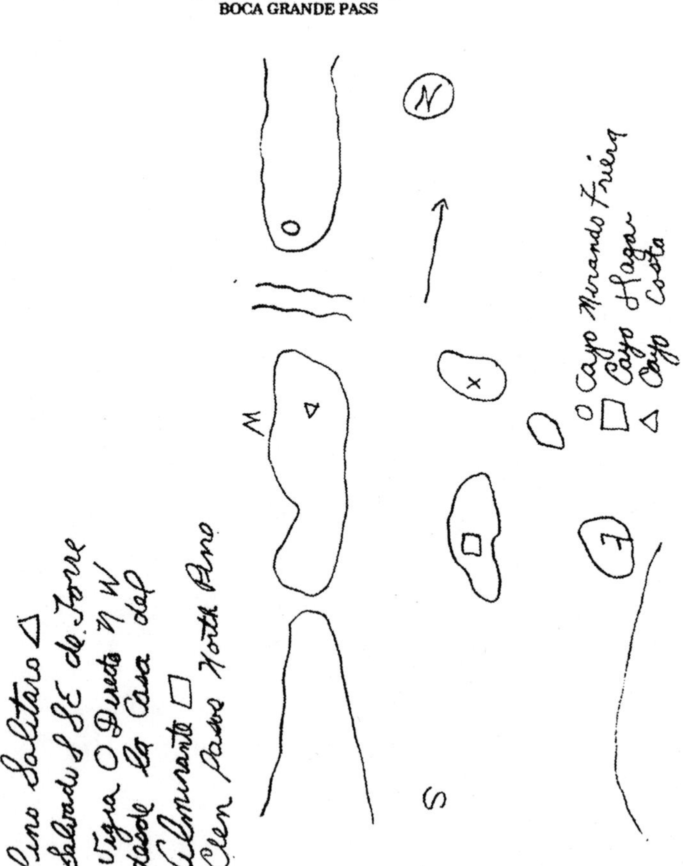

Of the people that I knew who spent much time looking for this Treasure, one really stands out. This person spent a lot of time doing research to determine which island the house of the "Admiral" had been located and this fellow was really obsessed by this TX. As time went by he began to believe that he really knew where the house had stood and the direction from the house to the place where the pine was to be found. It was easy to draw lines on maps and paper to the place where the Treasure is and yet another thing to follow this line through mangroves and dense underbrush. This fellow came up with the idea of creating his own trail, such as the "trail of crumbs" left in the fairy tale. Since this fellow was in the radio and TV repair business, his bright idea was to use old radio tubes dropped from a low flying plane from the shore on the heading and line to the Pine. With his large supply of tubes, a Piper Cup and someone to fly the plane, a mission was begun to create a simple way to get to the Treasure. After this bombing mission they went to the island thinking that they would simply walk on radio tubes right to the spot. Nice try. If my memory serves me correctly they found maybe a dozen tubes out of several hundred. It was not too long after this brain storm that his ambition for this TX began to fade.

The other person I had hunted treasure with, as he was the son of the "Colonel". Bob had once slipped onto Mondongo Island with the “Colonel” just to see what was there and had knowing that you needed permission from the owners never returned. Mondongo Island is owned by the Lykes Family and has long been a family retreat. After some effort on his part, Bob got permission from either Charley Lykes or Chester Ferguson to take his detectors to the island and look. Bob told me that he spent a lot of time looking over the island and never found anything and that he was disappointed. I have hunted with Bob and I don’t really think he spent much time looking. He did say that there at one time must have been a really large mound on the island but it had been dug away similar to what had happened at the “Cash Mound”. There is a rumor that a large treasure was retrieved from this mound in the late 1800’s and could have helped in the funding to establish the family fortune.

My personal pick for the island of the “House of the Admiral” is Patricia Island. My main reason is the depth of the water. Around both Useppa and Mondongo the water depth is much too shallow to handle vessels with the draft that the pirates had. Maybe 50 feet West of Patricia Island there is a channel with water 10 to 12 feet deep and this channel runs directly into Charlotte Harbor. This depth is plenty deep to handle the draft of a pirate ship. I have been on Patricia Island but have never worked a detector there as I had nothing to base a search on. There is plenty of evidence of human habitation. There was a concrete cistern, fruit trees (one of the largest Key Lime trees, covered in fruit, that I had ever seen), St. Augustine grass on which fed an abundance of Gopher turtles. The place where it appeared the house stood was on the highest point of the island. On the treasure map the island with the square is probably Useppa and the island with the X is Patricia, as Patricia is closest to the open water.

PORTUGESE CHART

In the past, I had in my possession, a Portugese chart dated 1513 of Tampa Bay and its accuracy was almost unbelievable. I have compared it with the 1879 Coast and Geodetic chart of Tampa Bay, the first one published by the U.S. Government, for the navigation of the bay. The water depths, all done with a lead line, were almost exactly the same and if an overlay could have been done, all the rest would have been just as accurate. If this chart was dated 1513, that was when the cartographer finished, my question would be, when were the Portugese here to do the exploration of Tampa Bay.

A lot of credit is given to named explorers i.e. DeSoto, DeNarves, Columbus, etal, for all of their discoveries but it appears based on the date of this chart that they all probably dropped by the "Map

Store" in Lisbon and picked up the latest chart for their own expeditions.

This chart was not only of the waters of the bay but also went a half a mile or so inland. This chart was so accurate that it depicted the two large artesian wells that flowed on the South end of the Pinellas peninsula, one at 31st Street and the other at 14th Street where they met the bay.

The islands of the bay were well marked and had the same shape as the ones shown on the C & G S chart. With no basic change in 350 years between the charts, the amount of change in the last 100 years, gives one concern as to what man has done to this area.

The Pirates who frequented this area and who based their operations on the West Coast of Florida, all had some connection with Portugal and possibly located here deliberately, based on the knowledge of the un-named Portuguese explorers who mapped the area before them.

There probably is much more history about Pirates and Explorers connected with Tampa Bay and the West Coast of Florida but due to local biases and historians wanting to put forth their own agenda, it will be lost forever.

A local man, Mercer Brown, had an extensive collection of charts and I believe the copies that I had were from this collection. These maps and charts were donated to the University of Florida by him and can be found in the P. K. Yonge Library of Florida History.

COCKROACH MOUND

My treasure hunting buddy, Al, had long believed that there was treasure on the Cockroach Indian Mound, on the East side of Tampa Bay. There have been rumors that a small treasure was taken from the mound in 1939. There was, supposedly on this same spot, was some sort of light marker for night navigation on the bay, this being sometime in the early 1800's.

In 1957, Al made arrangements to borrow a 16 foot row boat with a 7 ½ horsepower outboard motor. This boat belonged to Robert Eady and was not in the greatest condition. It leaked some and the bottom had a goodly amount of barnacles.

On a nice Sunday morning we left Little Bayou in the boat, taking with us our old "GI" detectors, lunch and mosquito spray. This old boat might have been able to do 5 mph and the distance across the bay from point to point is about 10 miles. On this morning the bay was nice and calm and we got to the other side about 11 AM.

Once we got inside of Cockroach Bay everything looked the same and we could not make out where the mound was even with its considerable height. We shut the engine off and in the distance we could hear what sounded like a radio playing some kind of music. Following the sound, with the hope of getting directions to the mound, we pressed on. While following a small channel towards the sound we saw a small shack, a ways back from the shore and there was the source of the music. Tying off to a small dock I proceeded towards the shack. When I got to within about 50 feet of the shack an old man burst out the door with a shotgun, a really bad temper and started demanding to know what I was doing on his property. With that big shotgun pointed at me, I had a feeling that this was not going to be a good day. With my best "crackerese" I explained that we were just looking for directions on how to get to the Cockroach Mound. Without ever taking the shotgun off of me, he told me what marks to follow to get there and to never bother him again while he was listening to his religious programs. I assured him that we would never disturb him again and headed for the boat. Al and Robert both said that they thought that I was a dead man for sure.

1879
Coast Chart No.177
Tampa Bay
Indian Hill (Cockroach Mound)

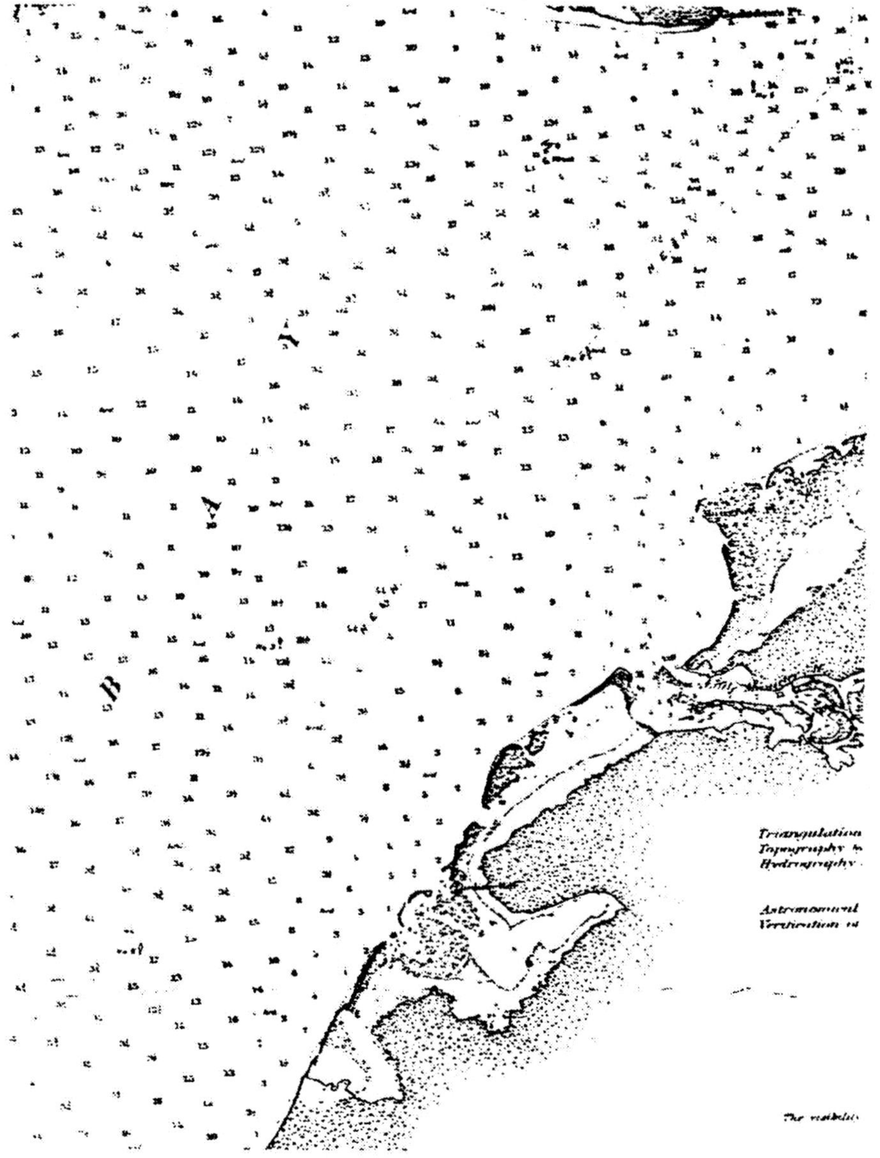

The old man did give good directions, we did as he instructed and in a little while we came to the mound. This mound is quite large and the highest part is close to the bay on its West side, at the mid part of the mound towards the East it drops off to maybe half the height of the tallest part. A few hours were spent looking over the highest part of the mound as it was free of almost any undergrowth and the easiest part to work the detectors. There was evidence that others had been there as there were small holes dug all over. My only treasure was a old silver spoon that had seen better days. The lower part of the mound on the East side was very grown over and we did not have the time to clear it enough to use the detectors. After this trip my research discovered this East side is where the Smithsonian had a dig in the 1920's and this side is where the burials were. The taller West side was probably ceremonial. It is some time in the 1920's the Smithsonian did their small dig here, mainly on the East side down below the highest part. It is said that a small treasure was taken from the highest part of the mound in 1939 by parties unknown.

In the afternoon a strong wind began to blow from the Southeast and as it was nearly 4 o'clock we decided it really was time to head back across the bay. The shallow water near shore, was relatively calm but as we moved towards the middle part of the bay and into the deeper water it began to be very rough. By us going to the West and the wind coming from the Southeast it caused it to be a following wind. This old boat did not have much of a transom and some of almost every wave was getting into the boat and besides that it also drowned out the motor. Robert was operating the motor so it was his responsibility to keep it running. This motor was probably as old as the boat and the way to start it was by a rope start that you had to rewind by hand with each pull. Al and I had to keep bailing the water out or we would without a doubt, sink. Besides having to worry about the boat sinking, the motor not running and us having no life preservers, now we were in the middle of the ship channel and the next thing I could envision was getting run over by some large ship. Al and I discovered that if we both bailed the water from the front of the boat the motor and transom did not take as much water, which cut down on how many times we restarted the motor and how much water we bailed. After what felt like an eternity we made it to shallower water and as the size of the waves got less, we finally made it back into Little Bayou at dark. What had taken two hours to do in the morning had taken four hours to do in the afternoon.

This treasure hunting sometimes causes a person to do strange, stupid and dangerous things. I have never returned to the Cockroach Mound.

PICNIC GROUNDS

There has long been a story about a Pirate vessel being chased up into Tampa Bay by some Government ship. The Pirate steered into a bay that is now just North of the St. Pete/Clearwater Airport. Even though there is fairly deep water in this part of the bay there was only a small channel leading into it. The Pirate obviously knew how to navigate the channel to get to the deep water and the Government boat did not. It is said the Government boat sat on the outside and shelled the Pirate until the ship was set afire. The crew supposedly took the treasure, abandoned the burning ship and buried the treasure on the shore and disappeared.

The area where the crew buried the treasure used to be called the "Picnic Grounds". My grandmother told me she used to go there as a child on picnics. She said it was a beautiful bluff, a place with large, shady oaks and a sandy beach. This place is now located behind the Clearwater Mall and is now occupied by condominiums.

At the time I was treasure hunting, I was employed as a pilot for Aerovias Sud Americana, a small cargo airline operating out of St. Pete/Clearwater Airport. One of our captains was a member of the McMullen family, a family that settled this area in around 1848. He lived about ½ a mile South of the "Picnic Grounds" on the West end of the bay. We were on a trip together and knowing that I had this interest in treasure hunting related to me the following story.

When he was around 10 years old, a large boat came into the bay and was towing a barge with a crane on it. He noticed that the crew went ashore at the "Picnic Grounds". Not knowing what was going on and with the curiosity of a young boy, he went to see what they were up to. He said he never really asked but merely watched. He offered to bring them cold water to drink and they accepted his offer. For several days this went on with Terry suppling these men with cold water and him watching what was going on. He said he did not see the men dig or really do much of anything. A few mornings after this bunch came to the bay Terry looked out and saw that the boat, barge and crane were gone. Wondering what was left behind, he returned to the bluff and there he found a hole dug beneath a large oak tree. In the hole all there was left was an impression of what could have been a chest.

The location of where this Pirate sank is probably where one of the McMullens when poling his boat between Bayview and their homestead, hit something with the pole. He took the time to sound out the length of whatever it was and it seemed to be a ship of more than 50 feet. He nor anyone else I know of has ever attempted to find out what was sunk there. If it is the Pirate, she is still probably with her canons but not much else.

WALL IN EVERGLADES

I realize that this story has nothing to do with treasure but in all reality the search is the best part of hunting treasures and finding it, anti-climatic. Just solving the mystery is a part of human nature and I do wish finding the "TX" was as easy as finding this wall.

We had for many years heard a story about a wall in the Everglades and most of it was connected to the legend of Atlantis. Along with this wall was supposed to be a pyramid with just the top of it sticking up out of the mud.

Frank Hudson, a spinner of many a tall tale, told us that he had found a man in Immokalee who knew where it was and could take us to see it. Having serious doubts as to Frank's story and this wall, we asked him to set up a meeting to have this person take us to the wall.

Frank did set up a meeting and in March 1968 we went to Immokalee to meet a person named Frank Brown, at the feed store, who was a life long resident of Immokalee and about 70 years of age and was supposed to have the location and could take us to the wall.

Frank, still being an active person, wanted to take us to where the wall was and to see it again for himself. He said that he had seen the wall when he was hunting alligators with his wife in around 1926 and had not been back there since. Frank told the story of since his wife was a Seminole Indian, he was given the opportunity to become a "Blood Brother" to the Seminole Tribe and according to Frank, the only white man to have been given the honor. When Frank was hunting this land Florida was a "free range" state with no fences and now almost all land is fenced.

Frank said he could surely return to the wall but would not do so until he had permission of the owner. A phone call was made to the owner, who said that even he had heard of a wall in the area and since it was on his property and he had never seen it he would like to see it, so he granted us the permission to get on his property. The owner met us at a gate in front of his ranch and in his Ford Bronco we passed the first locked gate of several on our way to the wall. Frank seemed to have an uncanny sense of direction, as all these fences and gates were put in long after he was here and yet he seemed to know exactly where to go. Frank directed us in the direction of what he called a "pop ash" pond and said that is the place that he and his wife were hunting alligators and that the wall was just on the other side. Parking the Bronco we walked around the pond as Frank directed and just as he said, there was the wall. About two weeks later another group went back to the area, led by a person who was in on the first trip and without the owners knowledge, tried to make it back to the wall. They were unsuccessful and I don't believe anybody has been to the wall since. There are now probably not 10 people alive who have seen this wall.

One thing for sure this wall has no connection to the Atlantis story. The wall is about 4 feet high, 2-3 feet across and maybe 100 feet long. It is made of limestone rocks, fitted together, using no concrete or mortar. There are no curves or corners and who put it there or why may never be known. This writers guess is that it was put up by U. S. Army soldiers for some kind of fortification during the second Seminole Indian War and there probably are no pyramids to be found.

The wall is not very far West of the Big Cypress Indian Reservation.

Frank Brown (with hat)

Wall in Everglades

BOURNE ISLAND

We have spent much time looking for this island referred to in the "Papers" and I do believe it is the long island that separates Gasparilla Bay from Lemon Bay. The South end of the island would make it be in Gasparilla Bay and be close to the South end of Little Gasparilla Island where the "killing ground" was supposed to be. The "papers" say that the $6,000,000 was buried on the south end.

We have researched and can find no information that identifies or locates where this island was to be found. The 1879 chart of Charlotte Harbor has no islands by this name. A number of 1700 charts also show no island by this name and could be a name given to it by the pirates themselves. Research reveals that the name could, according to Webster, mean in medieval English a spring, brook or stream or in ancient French a limit or boundary. The island that forms the "narrows" referred to in the "papers" can fit any or all these meanings. This island is very close to where the treasure was at Cape Haze and also the Jewel Pond.

I had heard of a mast yoke with the brass knobs on top that was seen on Palm Island and it was seen on its South end. This island used to have a bridge to it but it was removed when the Intercoastal Waterway was put in and now the only way to the island is by boat. These yokes were purportedly seen where the mangroves and the higher ground met and where it should have been if it was there as a mark for the treasure mentioned in the "papers" and this is Bourne Island. There are many stories that say that there were treasures buried that used mast yokes as a mark. The "papers" never mention mast yokes in reference to this treasure. We did spend a lot of time looking for these mast yokes as the information did come from a fairly reliable source.

On our first trip we did not take our detectors as we believed that, as I was told, the yokes were sticking above the ground and the machines were not necessary. We spent most of the day searching the high tide line and found nothing that gave us any optimism. The only thing missing was that nobody had dug any holes, so if anything were here it wasn't dug up. We felt that maybe someone by chance had found the yoke and not knowing what it marked, removed it just for its antiquity.

We later returned with the detectors to search the area and spent much of the day looking where we believe that if the mast yoke had been here where it most likely would have been. We were never able to get any readings with the machines after what we thought was a thorough search and decided that more information was needed before doing it again.

It is possible that if the mast yoke were really there, we did not go far enough into the mangroves. There are now many condos on the island and I don't know what the South end looks like today but with the State of Florida protecting the mangroves the way they are, it might just still be there.

EPILOGUE

I don't believe that there is anyone who is not a treasure hunter at heart. Be it only in finding treasure in old comic books or to the discovery of a rare painting, the excitement is still the same. The finding of treasure is still a state of mind.

I have resisted in sharing or making this diary public for a long time but the time has come for me to share the excitement of reading such an unique diary. Time changed the landscape little from when the diary was written to when I was privileged to search for the very same elusive treasures and but now 40 years later almost all these places now have expensive homes or condominiums on them.

It is now my pleasure to share this part of Florida's past with the reader.

About the Author:

P. T. Meharg

The Author was born in St. Petersburg, Florida in 1936. His mother was born in Seminole, Florida in 1906 and who's father settled there in 1880. The Author's father was born in Richmond, Virginia and came to St. Petersburg in 1923 and he had a keen interest in history, especially the Civil War and the American Indians. The Author's father, at an early age, interested him with artifacts found by the his father at battle sites in and around Richmond, musket balls, slugs, arrow heads and even a brick from the Appomattox Court House. On family vacation trips, would take the Author to his favorite locations and would find more artifacts. The Author's grandfather created in him his real interest in the history of Florida's West coast, with stories told to him about the Spanish he had dug up, the Indians he had seen and all of the interesting places along the West coast. The Author still hunts for lost money and jewels, but now it is at the beach, with both an underwater detector and one for up the beach and still finds enough valuables to enjoy the hunt.

The Author has a diverse background of interests having been an Airline pilot, President and originator of a Marine Coatings paint company, manufacturing anti-fouling coatings and owner and operator of a yacht maintenance service and today is semi-retired.

Printed in the United States
1389500005B/1-63